THE
HABIT BREAKER

HOW TO CHANGE FOR GOOD

EMS HANCOCK

RIVER
PUBLISHING

River Publishing & Media Ltd
Bradbourne Stables
East Malling
Kent ME19 6DZ
United Kingdom

info@river-publishing.co.uk

ISBN 978-1-908393-68-5
Cover design by www.spiffingcovers.com
Printed in the United Kingdom

Contents

What Others Are Saying...

"Ems' writing always beautifully blends wisdom, personal vulnerability and research with her humour and God-given revelation. *The Habit Breaker* is no exception."
Ian Henderson, CEO and founder of Visible (visibleministries.com)

"I can recommend this book firstly because I know the author, and she lives what she speaks about. But also because we need to hear what she has to say about breaking free from harmful habits, which we all succumb to from time to time. The practical questions in each chapter are ideal for personal study or group work."
Debra Green OBE, Founding Director of ROC (roc.uk.com)

"This encouraging, challenging and practical read will help you break the habits that hold you back – and help you take up some that will positively push you forward. Buy it, read it and live it."
Gavin Calver, Director of Missions, Evangelical Alliance (www.eauk.org)

"Deeply honest, practical and engaging, The Habit Breaker will help you and those you love break bad habits and discover how to live in hope and freedom."
Katharine Hill, UK Director, Care for the Family

"If you have longed and longed for a key to set yourself or someone close to you free, you just found it in the shape of this book. *The Habit Breaker* provides the rationale for the

changes we all need to make, and is a playbook to access the power to make them possible."
Anthony Delaney, Leader, Ivy Network

"Ems Hancock is quite simply one of the most talented people I know. Here she brings her unique talent for the written word to the challenging and vital topic of our habits. I truly believe that our habits determine our future and ultimately our destiny. That means you are probably holding in your hands the most important book you've looked at for a very long time."
Andy Hawthorne OBE, Founder and Chief Executive of The Message Trust

"We are creatures of habit and Ems' new book is a must-read for anyone who is struggling with long term or early stage habits. Ems writes with a mix of vulnerability and authority, and shares her wisdom on the subject with her usual humour and grace. Another consistently brilliant read."
Lily-Jo, Counsellor and Founder of The Lily-Jo Project (www.thelilyjoproject.com)

Dedication

WITH MADLY ENORMOUS AMOUNTS OF THANKS:
I am hugely grateful for my friend Ian Henderson (Founder and CEO of Visible Ministries) who has walked through this book with me, inputting his wisdom and skillfully questioning and adding to my ideas.

This book is dedicated to two other precious friends who have faithfully journeyed alongside me so closely for the past year:

Mary Brewood and Rachel Bedicer,
Thank you for being with me when Jericho fell xxx

Acknowledgements

I praise you, Father God, that You have won every battle we will ever face.

Grateful thanks to my wonderful publisher and friend, Tim Pettingale, for letting me write what God puts on my heart.

Thank you to my amazing family: my husband, Jon, for all your love and support. Thank you to our children, Sam, Ben, Tom and Esther, for understanding how important and healing this has been for me.

Thank you to Ian and Jen Henderson for consistently loving me, praying for me and championing me.

I have huge love for all my pals at Ivy. Thank you to each of you for your cheerleading.

Big love to our beautiful Grow Group, especially Ric and Rach, who consistently breathe life into my dreams.

And huge thanks to my Ninjas, without whom I would be much less daring.

Finally, thank you to my mentor and friend, Beryl Craig, who has taught me so much and helped me to dig so much deeper into the Bible this year.

A Little Note From Ems...

Hello.

Firstly, "Well done!"

Well done for choosing to read a book that examines your habits. I salute you. I know it's not an easy topic, so I thought I would promise to keep checking up on you as we journey through the pages.

These, "How are you doing?" times will offer you a pause in the writing to think, process, and work out what God is saying to you and what you might want to say back. These are times to make yourself a drink and sit still for a bit.
If at all possible, please don't skip over these sections.

Abraham Lincoln is famously quoted as saying, "Give me six hours to chop down a tree and I will spend the first four sharpening the axe."

My prayer is that this book will help you sharpen your axe in order to chop down the trees that you need to fell. The temptation will be to read something and then get busy trying to cut stuff down. But you might need to stop a while and think things through; to test the blade from time to time and check your heart a bit. Don't race through the text trying to get to the end. You will get much more out of the whole experience if you pace yourself. Try to pay attention to what you are feeling. And keep asking the Holy Spirit what He is doing in you.

Go slow.

And, just so we understand each other – in no way am I sitting here tapping away at my laptop in any sanctimonious way, judging you for not getting yourself together. If you could see some of the hideous messes I have been through in my life, it might be the other way round – you might be tempted to judge me.

I am writing this book because I understand what it is like to have habits that are really destructive. Having to face who I really was when no one else was looking has been painful for me. I know how hard it is to wade through the internal script of my mind and have to destroy reams of my own bad press.

I get it.

I never want you to forget that I am FOR you in this whole process.

So let's make a deal. I will be really honest with you in this book and tell you some of the stuff I have gone though and been freed from, and you can start to work through some of yours. Okay?

Cheering you on as you begin,
Ems

Cutting the Strings

"The chains of habit are too light to be felt
until they are too heavy to be broken."
–Anon

One morning as I walked home from dropping my children off at school, I caught sight of a woman wearing one of the saddest T-shirt slogans I have ever seen. Her top said,
"It gets no better."
Unsurprisingly, the T-shirt was grey. And so, by the looks of things, was the woman's mood.

I wanted to stop her in the street, look her in the eyes and say, "Yes it does!"

I felt myself getting emotional as I imagined holding her hands and saying to her, "Take off that shirt. It's a lie! Life holds so much more for you than this! You don't have to carry on feeling such despair, or believing that everything is going to be downhill from now on!"

Can you imagine a more hopeless thing to wear?

I honestly can't.

But so many of us carry that kind of despondent bumper sticker in our hearts.

We may not advertise it on our clothing, but this is the attitude swimming around in the murk of our minds. We have tried and failed. We have grown weary. We have settled. We have seen no change. So we have simply given up.

In opposite circumstances, when we are really, truly happy, we might say,

"It doesn't get any better than this!"

Somehow this phrase is a sign of our contentment. But can you see that this too is a kind of self-curse and a definite lie?

For the Christian, life constantly holds the capacity to get better. All the time. Because we are all moving towards more growth, more understanding, and more wisdom. Even if what we are going through now is downright awful, God can still bring good things out of it.

I have always believed that my best is yet to come. I don't think that my most successful, happy and wonderful days are in my past. I would be miserable if I thought that! I know that I have more excitement, creativity, fulfilment, hope and joy ahead of me. And I believe that for you too. I believe it because it says so in the Bible.

1 Corinthians 2:9 (NLT) explains that,

"No eye has seen, no ear has heard, and no mind has imagined what God has prepared for those who love him."

In other words, if you love God you have no idea how amazing your life is going to get! You can't even imagine it!

God has some beautiful things prepared for those of us who love Him.

You may have started this book because you feel stuck in a rut, caught up in things that you despise but don't know how to free yourself from. You may be feeling rubbish and guilty about some of those habits and even wondering if they have stopped God from loving you and blessing you.

You are not alone.

But you are not correct.

I have never met a single person who did not struggle with a bad habit of some kind. And I have met many, many others who do their very best to hide all their vices and foibles and hope no one ever finds them out.

You might be doubting that you really can change the patterns of a lifetime. You might question whether you can ever break destructive habits and cultivate new, healthy ones.

The Habit Breaker is for anyone in that place. It is for those who feel as though things can never change for them or those they love. It's for those who regularly hang their heads and think they are total losers.

Because that is not actually the truth.

Whatever situation you are in, you can know forgiveness, change, peace and contentment. You can experience the joy of true liberty that only Jesus gives. It is never too late. This book contains a number of powerful stories of people of different ages and backgrounds who have found that freedom for themselves.

I believe in that freedom. Passionately. In fact, I am also living proof of it.

Having experienced breakthrough in my life and in the lives of those around me, I know that even the worst and most damaging of habits are no match for the incredible power of the living God!

I can't keep that kind of thing to myself. I have to share what I have found and, more importantly, WHO I have found to be the rescuer and freedom fighter of my soul.

J.C. Ryle wrote, "Habits of good or evil are daily strengthening your hearts. Every day you are either getting nearer to God or further off."

So which is it for you? Honestly?

The habits you choose today will determine to a great extent the person you will be tomorrow. Are you ready to break those habits that hurt you and begin ones that will set you and others free?

The scissors are waiting.

I believe it is time for you to cut those strings.

Chapter 1
Wired To Want

"Consider what man is. He is a creature that desires happiness, and cannot but desire it. The desire of happiness is woven into his nature, and cannot be eradicated. It is as natural for him to desire as it is to breathe."
–Thomas Boston

The bluebottle buzzed annoyingly into the room. Like a badly-behaved drunk at a party, it announced its unwelcome presence by zipping past me loudly, a number of times. It then repeatedly hit the windowpane next to my desk, over, and over again. The low-pitched revving slowly began to wind me up. I tried to ignore it and carry on writing. But it was insistently loud. Struggling to concentrate, I eventually sighed, stood up and opened the window. After a few more minutes of head banging (mine, as well as the fly's) out it flew. My peace was restored.

Like that troublesome insect, there are some behaviour patterns in each of us that we (or others) can find unpleasant or unhealthy. There are things we repeatedly do, either in private or public, that confuse or annoy us or make us feel beaten down. These habits make us feel trapped, ashamed and unable to change.

Maybe you know what that looks like? Perhaps there is

something you have done today that you already regret, and its only 8am?

You are in good company. Lean in.

Janine was a big lady. She did what my mother used to call "eat between snacks". She was an emotional eater too. If she broke a nail she needed a fry up to restore her. Janine was a member of the same "Weight Watchers" group as me in Liverpool, where I grew up. She would arrive and knock on the side door of the church hall because the front door was too small for her to get through. She needed two fire doors opening for her. She used to shout on arrival, "Hiya girls! Save me two chairs. One for each cheek!" To my knowledge the only pounds she lost was the registration money she faithfully gave our leader each week. Janine either stayed the same, or put on weight the whole time I knew her.

Maybe you know someone like her, or maybe you *are* someone like her. Perhaps you are living in an unhealthy pattern that you want to get out of, but you don't know how. Whatever your issue, whatever you want to be free from, I pray that this book will give you a head start. I am asking God to help you get an intoxicating view of your freedom as you read.

The mess of yes

We live in a world of "easy access". If we want something, the chances are someone makes it, offers it or sells it. Advertising noise surrounds us. Our radios, TVs and billboards tell us how to have whiter teeth, wider choices and whizzier broadband. Ever-increasing access to goods and services on the Internet means that everything we want is a click away, especially if we are willing to pay for it. We live in a world where people beep us at traffic lights because we have held them up for 1.2 seconds of their day. People are getting worse at waiting. We are surrounded by people with a warped sense of entitlement.

Our culture is all about the "drive through", "get it now", instant hit of gratification. Because we live in an, "I want it now" environment, we are constantly demanding more. We ask for something NOW and the reply is, "Yes, of course, would you like a large one?" We never say no to anything. And, crucially, no one ever says no to us.

This is not good for us. It doesn't teach us moderation, patience or self-control. In fact, when we do want to say no to something, we don't have the ability or the training or the language. It is simply not in our vocabulary or understanding.

This is the backdrop to our habit-forming. It is partly why many of us struggle to maintain good habits or make positive changes in our lives.

What is a habit?
The word "habit" can be defined as a regular tendency or practice that has become almost involuntary. (In other words, "I don't like it, but I can't help it"). A habit can be especially hard to give up because it thrives on repetition after a certain cue.

The word habit comes from the Latin *habitus* which means "condition, appearance, dress and attire". The root word also links back to the medical understanding of a person and how that person may be susceptible to disease or disorder. It also comes from the verb *habeo* meaning, "I have, hold or keep".

So the early useage of the word give us many clues about what our habits tell us. They demonstrate a great deal about the condition or state of a person. They often show us something of the health, or mind. They also give us an idea of what is important to that person and what they hold on to.

For the purposes of this book we will define good habits as those which give *health, life and peace to the body*. Perhaps then, we could say that a bad habit is a behaviour or practice that would be *detrimental to one's physical or mental health* –

and something that *robs us of peace*.

I would say that a bad habit isn't always an addiction – although it can definitely be the gateway to one.

What is an addiction?

What does an addiction look like? How would we define one? For me, addiction is simply "idolatry". It is putting something in the place of God. If you like, an addiction is a "worship disorder". I will explain more about what I mean later.

There are two main categories of addiction:

1. Substance addictions
2. Behaviour addictions

So what kinds of things can be addictive behaviours? What bad habits can we fall into?

The Bible identifies many things that lead us into unhelpful patterns of thinking and acting, such as complaining, over-eating, indulging, poor spending, gossip, malicious talk, gambling, wasting money, criticising others, over-work, self gratification and laziness.

Of course, there are other habits and dependencies that the Bible doesn't mention specifically – certain types of abuse, pornography, gaming, some forms of gambling, taking illegal drugs, having OCD, certain eating problems and smoking. (I will cover as many of these as I can in later chapters).

But this doesn't mean the Bible has nothing to say about these problems. Whilst it sometimes does not give an answer in terms of a chapter and verse we can quote, the heart of the way things are written and the general principles the Bible offers will aid people in many types of recovery. But a word of warning here: God uses His word to explain many things to us, but He still requires us to *"walk by faith, not by sight"* (2 Corinthians 5:7 KJV). That means receiving guidance from the Bible, listening to promptings from the Holy Spirit, and being guided by the advice and wisdom of godly leaders and friends.

There is great mystery in our faith. It is not meant to be formulaic. So please don't expect this book to be your "one size fits all" way out of your struggle and to answer every question you have. It can definitely help you, but it cannot do your changing or growing for you. You will have to want your recovery deeply and stay committed to your own journey. BUT, please know that I will be willing you on, all the way!

Habits aren't your label

When we become aware of our bad habits, dependencies or addictions we may notice ourselves starting to "wear" our issues as labels, saying phrases like...

"I am a drunk."

"I am an addict."

"I am fat."

"I am out of control."

...as though these were our NAMES and our identities.

I have learnt that my habits are not *who* I am. Just because I struggle with something doesn't mean I have *become* it. I have had terrible problems over the years with food. But this is not who I am. I am not a walking eating disorder. And nor, my friend, are you.

I find it hard when people say, "I am anorexic." I want to gently correct them and say "No, you HAVE anorexia." You might think that is a subtle, semantic difference. But isn't that how most lies start?

"But Ems," you might say "I *am* fat."

"No," I would disagree. "Some parts of your body may be fat, but you are not made up of fat and only fat are you? Therefore *you* are not fat. You *have* fat."

Your problems aren't who you are. You are so much more than the sum of your bad habits or your addictive tendencies or your wobbly bottom. And so, Praise the Living God, am I!

Like that fly I talked about earlier, some of us, desperately searching for an escape, end up feeling as though we are banging our head against a shut window. There are things we wish we didn't do, or didn't need. There are weaknesses we have that make us feel … well, weaker. But we *keep* doing them. We *keep* failing. We *keep* feeling the familiar patterns of shame and guilt. We try, and maybe even succeed for a while, but then we fail again. It can feel like the most vicious of circles. Especially because we have the added weight of feeling as though we ought NOT to have that very problem in the first place. We feel guilty because we *are* guilty. Then we feel guilty about that!

I will talk more about the negative cycles we can get into in Chapter 3, but first, I want us to understand why we form habits, in order for us to start to see how we can un-form or break them for good.

Craving in context

Sometimes without much warning, it will happen. Seemingly out of nowhere it will strike. The command, "GIVE ME SUGAR!" (or alcohol, junk food, a cigarette – insert your own issue) will claw its way into our brains. Then, as our minds catch up with our feelings, we will start to articulate that desire, need, or craving. That intense headline grips us repeatedly and won't let go until we GIVE IN. A while later, sometimes only seconds, we will feel some kind of guilt, remorse or question our behaviour. We will self-curse, self-deprecate, but deep down we know that we will do it…

All.

Over.

Again.

Does that sound like a familiar pattern to you?

Of course it does. Because we all operate in this way. All of us know what it is like to fall foul of a bad habit or be influenced by a substance of some kind – whether that be as innocuous as the innocent-looking custard cream or as dangerous and damaging as crack cocaine. Some of us will struggle more than others, but there will be at least one area of vulnerability in each of us.

Our cravings are hugely related to cues or context. Even though the desires we struggle with feel deep down and even base at times, conditioning and circumstance have a great deal to do with how they are played out.

Susan Albers, a psychologist at The Cleveland Clinic and author of *50 Ways to Soothe Yourself Without Food*, says that unlike physical hunger, which grows over the day, if we don't eat, our habitual cravings can appear to come out of the blue and "can be triggered by almost anything: stress, boredom, emotions or simply seeing or smelling a certain food."

We might not like that truth and we may even want to disagree with it. It may be that we are so used to our habits that we don't even notice them much any more, let alone see the need to change them. We have simply grown to accept them. They are part of us.

"This is just who I am," we say.

But is it?

We start to excuse or explain our behaviour and say it was handed down to us through our parents, or that an event triggered our habits, as if that means *there is nothing we can do about them*. We treat ourselves as though true freedom is not for us and we choose to just "live with" or underplay our issues.

I'm not being funny. Genuinely, I am not being at all funny. But is that the life you dreamed of? Settling for settling? Constantly feeling as though you are not truly free?

How are you doing?

Have a think for a minute about what you have just read. Look at the definition we used for "bad habits" for a moment. We said bad habits are:

Things that are detrimental to our physical or mental health and that rob us of peace.
Does that resonate with how you feel about your life right now?

What good habits do you practice?
Can you write them down?
How do those habits make you feel?

What habits would you say you currently struggle with?
Can you write them down?
How do those habits make you feel?

Did you find it hard to write either or both of those down?
Why do you think that is?

PRAY
Jesus, thank you that you understand me better than I understand myself. As I read this book, help me to hear your voice of love speaking over me. Thank you that you do not condemn me, but choose to forgive me for things I do wrong. Help me to live a life that pleases you and brings me deep fulfilment. Amen.

Warning about judging

Some of us can be quick to make judgements about others. We can start a dangerous game of comparing ourselves and our habits to someone else's traits or behaviour. We can say, "Well my problem with gambling is nowhere near as bad as his, so maybe I'm okay."

Or we say, "At least I don't have THAT issue" as though ours is somehow more palatable to God.

Matthew 7:1-5 in The Message version reads:

"Don't pick on people, jump on their failures, criticize their faults – unless, of course, you want the same treatment. That critical spirit has a way of boomeranging. It's easy to see a smudge on your neighbour's face and be oblivious to the ugly sneer on your own. Do you have the nerve to say, 'Let me wash your face for you,' when your own face is distorted by contempt? It's this whole travelling road-show mentality all over again, playing a holier-than-thou part instead of just living your part. Wipe that ugly sneer off your own face, and you might be fit to offer a washcloth to your neighbour."

That is strong stuff isn't it? As we can see here, the Bible is certain about how damaging it is to look at the issues of others before tackling our own. Some of the most broken people I have met are also the most rule-driven. They can be totally fixated on other people's problems and almost entirely ignorant of their own. Like having a blind spot in a car, they drive around, dangerously unaware of what it is they can't see, right in front of their faces.

Maybe you are one of those people. Perhaps you are someone who finds it very hard to see or deal with the problems in your own life, but you find it all too easy to criticise others. Perhaps you need to take some time out now, to sit and ask God what you are blind to in your own heart? It can be painful to look at our own failings, but in order for us to grow, it is very necessary and helpful.

Why are we wired to want?

Recently my Dad moved house. When we went to have a look round, we discovered that one of the overhead lights in the kitchen appeared to be wired into a plug socket light switch at floor level. It was permanently on at the wall and hidden behind a piece of furniture. It was both inconvenient and dangerous. The previous owners had apparently been content to live with the switch in this place for years.

Similarly, unless we allow a fresh pair of eyes on our lives, unless we choose to look at things in a different way, we can just carry on living with the inconvenience and danger of our cravings. We bend down to our lowest level, and allow that switch to control what we do and see.

Have you ever stopped and asked yourself why you crave something so badly that might not be good for you? On the surface of things it doesn't make sense to want to eat or drink something that will make you feel sick later, or put on so much weight that you will have to buy a bigger pair of jeans. Nor does it seem logical to want a drug that will damage you in some way. Isn't this just a bizarre form of self-harm?

The reason is that, like my Dad's house, each one of us has been wired very specifically and we are all turned on, or in some cases, "left on", by certain triggers and circumstances. To put it another way, we are a little like a TV on standby. Permanently ready to glare into life at the touch of a remote button, many of us have issues that are always "playing in the background", waiting to bombard us.

So what is it that we are really seeking deep down when we are craving something that's bad for us? We certainly aren't longing for the guilt we feel afterwards. We aren't hankering after another depressing trip to the store changing room where we squeeze ourselves into an outfit and then need help from an assistant peeling it off again. (Just me?) We aren't yearning for a closer look at the U-bend as we throw up after a binge session. Are we?

When we allow these things to happen, what are we really searching for? Scientists, theologians, psychologists and many experts agree that we are looking for one thing only: PLEASURE.

We are craving the pleasure we feel during our habit – the comforting buzz of the chocolate hitting the tongue, the sensation of the smoke filling the lungs, or the calming feeling of the alcohol soothing the troubled mind. That's why we do what we do. It's because we get pleasure and sometimes even relief from that part of the experience.

Now, I am not going to blind you with science. My scientific ability wouldn't be able to dazzle anyone anyway. For years I thought a Proton was a make of Japanese car. But I just want to explain (very simply) what is going on inside us when we are looking for happiness.

So, imagine you are now biting into a large, puffy sugary doughnut (or if you're not a fan of sweet things, imagine instead a homemade cheese scone ... or something/anything you can eat with unbridled joy).

Your brain gets a hit of dopamine, the main chemical associated with pleasure, and you feel, momentarily at least, a reward for your behaviour. Signals arrive in quick succession.

THIS TASTES AMAZING!

I NEEDED THAT!

MMMMM!

You may also feel other associated feelings of comfort, relief and relaxation. This physical sensation of reward is what we look for again and again. Interestingly, pleasure has the ability to block or mask other things. When we are experiencing something pleasurable, it helps us not remember the unpleasurable parts of our lives. For a short time it is as though they did not exist. Pleasure numbs our pain.

But dopamine is much more complex than this. It isn't just about getting a hit. It is a neurotransmitter that has many other brain functions too. Scientists are still researching all the ways it operates, but we know it is as diverse as controlling limb movement and also our attention span. It won't just kick in when we eat or drink, it increases when we tick off tasks or clean out a drawer. (Ah! This explains the sheer elation I get when tidying). It also comes into play when we create something. That's why some of us can feel real delight in DIY, baking or gardening.

Having low levels of dopamine can be a contributory factor in reaching out for something to cheer us up in the first place. So if life is hard we can have low dopamine levels, which means it's much easier to self-medicate and try to give ourselves a mental boost. It can lead us to search out coping mechanisms of all kinds, which can become bad habits, dependencies and addictions.

We are also craving a sense of being in control or dominion over something we like. It makes us feel powerful – even if only for a second. When we feel good, our body also releases another chemical called seratonin which is associated with feelings of wellbeing and control. Interestingly, eighty per cent of the body's seratonin levels are found in the stomach area. This is often why if we are hungry or thirsty, we are more grumpy and we won't make good decisions.

As Albert Einstein wisely said, "An empty stomach is not a good political adviser." And he was spot on wasn't he? It is well known in my family that you must NEVER ask me anything important if I am hungry. I will be unlikely to make any sense! Okay, so no more (almost) sciencey stuff for now…

First, let's take a closer look at the feeling of pleasure. Why is it that we are so obsessed with being happy?

Paula Hall says,

"In my years as a psychotherapist, I have found this to be undoubtedly true. It seems that we spend our whole existence longing to escape pain – physical, emotional and psychological – and crave pleasure. All my clients want to feel better. They seek respite from their pain and a solution to their unhappiness. Furthermore, they want to know how to be happy – and stay happy."

Our problem often comes when we find something that makes us happy, but the feeling it creates doesn't last. So we look to up the stakes (or in my case, STEAKS). We drink more, we eat more chocolate. We access more of whatever we want in order to find that elusive hit.

Pleasure-seekers

The word "pleasure" comes from the old French word *plaisir* meaning "to please". To understand a bit more about the need to please, I want to take you back to the start of humanity.

The Bible is clear that God created us with inbuilt needs and desires. In fact, we were designed by Him to want to be content and secure, and to want to please Him. He made us to crave relationship with Him, to need it and to benefit from it. For example Psalm 42:1-2 in the Amplified version says:

"As the deer pants [longingly] for the water brooks, so my soul pants [longingly] for You, O God. My soul (my life, my inner self) thirsts for God, for the living God."

In other words, we were made to yearn for God. Countless times we will read verses in the Bible that show us that a close relationship with God is good for our health, our wellbeing, our minds, our bodies, our relationships, our homes, our families, our businesses … in fact, good for every area of life.

Other things will give us pleasure, of course, but it won't be of the lasting, eternal kind and may have some pretty nasty side effects. Drinking alcohol is a good example.

Imagine you have a glass or two of your favourite tipple. You feel light hearted and light headed. You slap a few people on the back and laugh at nothing.

A few more glasses and you feel on top of the world. You start singing a song you know one line of, out of tune, and telling people you've never met before that you love them and will never leave them. You ask them their names and then don't listen to the answer – because you are still singing, "Come on Eileen! Da da da da da da!" over and over again.

Then you start swaying and eventually pass out at a bus stop. Somehow you find your way home. You leave a neighbour the unwelcome and unsightly gift of a "lawn pizza". Then the following day you wake, suffering with the mother and father of all hangovers. Your mouth feels like the bottom of a birdcage. You are dehydrated and desperate for a quiet, dark room to sleep in. You throw up again. You feel imbalanced and ill. You feel very sorry for yourself and wonder if that seventh pint was a good idea. For many people a good night out on the town is followed by a bad day in – in a dressing gown!

God wants to give us joy that has no negative backlash, no hangover, no bad side effects. Very few earthly pleasures can give us that promise and NONE offer it to us forever. Let's look at a scripture from Psalm 16:5-11 (GNT)

"You, Lord, are all I have, and you give me all I need; my future is in your hands. How wonderful are your gifts to me; how good they are! I praise the Lord, because he guides me, and in the night my conscience warns me. I am always aware of the Lord's presence; he is near, and

nothing can shake me. And so I am thankful and glad, and I feel completely secure, because you protect me from the power of death. I have served you faithfully, and you will not abandon me to the world of the dead. You will show me the path that leads to life; your presence fills me with joy and brings me pleasure forever."

This scripture, especially the last line, blew me away! Did you miss it? Maybe read it again. It says that only God can show us the path that leads to life. Only His presence can fill us with joy and *bring us pleasure forever*. If we please Him, we, in turn will be pleased. The simple fact is: *pleasing God makes us truly, lastingly happy.*

Now, slow down here because this is a biggie. One of the most audacious lies of the enemy involves disguising this truth. The devil will consistently try and paint God as a *kill-joy* – someone who stops us having fun and enjoying life. The media often portrays Christians as being miserable, double-minded, dull and boring. (Or crazy lunatics who obsess about minutiae, but who aren't earthed in reality). When actually the truth is that God is the ultimate *fill-joy* and following Him is the best way to live. Being with Him literally tops us up with happiness and contentment. Authentic Christians are the happiest people on earth!

But our trouble is that we look for the satisfaction and pleasure found in God in all the wrong places. Rather than "pleasing Him" we look for ways to "please ourselves", thinking this will make us happy. We try and manufacture pleasure in other ways. We look to be pleased by our box sets, our unusual garden ornaments, our expensive foreign holidays, our latest hobbies and all manner of other poor substitutes. But all of those things have something in common.

They are *temporary*.

THEN, as if this isn't bad enough, when we still aren't

happy we decide that we now need to try to please other people. We think that will hit the spot. So we look for people to please and have a good go. We rush around, trying to fulfil other people's expectations of us. But this doesn't make us happy either. In fact, most of the time it leads to us being very unhappy indeed.

Many people's lives are such a wreck because *they are looking for permanent pleasure outside of something permanent.* Dissatisfaction and unhappiness in life is the ugly, deep root of all kinds of distressing behaviour. It is why people cheat on their spouses, why families are broken and why so many abuse drugs. It is why people mindlessly binge on fast food and waste hours glued to the TV. It is why thousands endlessly paw through social media sites and why whole days feel pointlessly stolen from their lives.

We all have inner yearnings, but because we don't sit in stillness, we mishear, misread or misunderstand what we need. The world tells us that if we just get that new phone or that more muscular husband, we will be happier. Or perhaps if we get some better qualifications and make more money, we will be more satisfied. We have been truly duped! Until we know why we were made and what we were made for, lots of things can feel disjointed and disconnected.

Let me make a bold statement.

Deep down, you are not looking for a better job or better pay or a better home. At least, that is not what you actually need. What you need and what you are really looking for is a more intimate relationship with God. Because this is how you were wired and why you were made.

Rick Warren says,

"You were made by God and for God and until you understand that, life will never make sense."

I hope, and I pray, that if you have never realised this before, you will understand it now: You cannot ever be truly happy outside of a deep relationship with your Father.

In *Thoughts on Good and Evil,* St. Nicholas of Serbia wrote:

"If a person wants to get an idea about the pyramids of Egypt, he must either trust those who have been in immediate proximity to the pyramids, or he must get next to them himself. There is no third option. In the same way a person can get an impression of God: He must either trust those who have stood and stand in immediate proximity to God, or he must take pains to come into such proximity himself."

Have you ever come into proximity with God? Have you ever taken time to try to find Him or get to know Him?

I trust and pray that this book will help you on your journey. In fact, why not ask Him now? You could pray this prayer before you read on:

"Lord, You know how I feel right now. You know that I have been searching for happiness and contentment in things that aren't lasting and satisfying long-term. Forgive me for trying to please myself, or others. From now on, help me to work out how to please you. Teach me your ways and help me live a life that is free from addiction and dependency. Amen."

If you prayed that prayer, please tell someone you know and trust who is a Christian. Or, feel free to get in touch with me via my website. (www.emshancock.com) You just made a brand new start! Well done!

Upside-down happiness

We have already said that God created us with a craving to be happy. But it is not a happiness that the world understands or gives. It is an upside-down-rule-breaking happiness that can even be happy in the midst of despair and crisis. It is the most potent and powerful happiness there is, because it is not based on our circumstances or feelings or our hairstyle. Indeed, it would not be godly, feel godly, or look like godliness if it were. It is more than worldly happiness. God's plans for us are bigger than mere contentment. They are more about deep and lasting joy. James 1:2-4 (TLB) says:

"Dear brothers, is your life full of difficulties and temptations? Then be happy, for when the way is rough, your patience has a chance to grow. So let it grow, and don't try to squirm out of your problems. For when your patience is finally in full bloom, then you will be ready for anything, strong in character, full and complete."

God knew what He was doing when He made us to seek pleasure in Him. He understood that creating us in this way would align us to Him more closely and make us crave His company more. He wants us, as this verse puts it, "ready for anything, strong in character, full and complete."

Guess what? All of the side effects of craving God are good for us, and good for others. We become less selfish, less self-absorbed and more self-controlled. We see the world with new eyes. We are not impressed and swayed by the things that impress others. We are not fooled by fakeries and forgeries. We are free, joyful and full of hope. I absolutely 100 per cent want that kind of life.

How about you?

I'm already Christian, shouldn't I now be free of bad habits?

I have been asked this question a number of times. I am sorry to be a harbinger of gloom, but just because you are a devout Christian doesn't mean you won't ever succumb to the lure of addictions. Even though you love Jesus, you can still be tempted to do things that are unhealthy, ungodly and unwise.

I am a big fan of prayer ministry and have seen God

totally heal and restore people through the power of prayer. But I would never expect to say to someone battling with alcoholism, "Well, just say a prayer and all your problems will go away." We need to remember that addictions affect our emotions and our minds. They impact our bodies and our hearts. God is an holistic God who wants the whole of us to be free. This may take various amounts of therapy, time, prayer or support. We will chat more about this later in the book. The wonderful news is that God totally understands how we feel and all the issues life throws at us. Read this passage that the apostle Paul wrote to the Christians in Rome way back in AD 56-57.

"I've tried everything and nothing helps. I'm at the end of my rope. Is there no one who can do anything for me? Isn't that the real question? The answer, thank God, is that Jesus Christ can and does. He acted to set things right in this life of contradictions where I want to serve God with all my heart and mind, but am pulled by the influence of sin to do something totally different." Romans 7:24-25 (The Message)

I find it so comforting that the Bible is so up-to-date, honest and real about how we will feel sometimes. We don't have to hide who we are or how we are doing with God. He knows the things that pull us and influence us.

In fact, 1 Corinthians 10:13 (ESV) tells us that,

"No temptation has overtaken you that is not common to man. God is faithful, and he will not let you be tempted beyond your ability, but with the temptation he will also provide the way of escape, that you may be able to endure it."

God is faithful. He will help us when we struggle. In fact, did you notice that in this verse it tells us that it is *Him* who provides the escape route? He gives us the power to break our bad habits *before* they break us. We will discuss some of the ways in which He helps us to do this in the coming chapters.

You may well have habits still present in your life that pre-date you finding Jesus. The good news is that God loves us way before we become perfect. Which is great, because NONE of us ever will be, this side of glory!

In fact, the Bible assures us that, *"God demonstrates his own love for us in this: While we were still sinners, Christ died for us."* (Romans 5:8 NIV)

God loves you now, whether you smoke or whether you don't. He loves you whether you have a gambling problem, or if you eat in between meals, or if you starve yourself. He loves you if you access Porn. He loves you if you cut yourself. He loves you if you hate every single fibre of your being.

He doesn't love you because you are loveable or because you deserve it. He doesn't love you because you give to charity, or work hard or love your kids. He doesn't love you because you recycle or read great Christian books on the bus. He loves you because it is His nature. He doesn't just love you, He *embodies* love. The Bible tells us He IS love (1 John 4:8 and 16). Nothing can stop Him loving you because it is WHO HE IS.

Amazingly, we also know that God doesn't heap condemnation and guilt on us when we do mess up.

Romans 8:1 says,

"Therefore, there is now no condemnation for those who are in Christ Jesus, because through Christ Jesus the law of the Spirit who gives life has set you free from the law of sin and death."

That's a lot to think about I know.

But isn't it good news to remember that even right now with a bin full of chocolate wrappers or a handbag stuffed with cigarettes, you are loved, totally and completely?

I think so too.

How are you doing?

Which of the verses you have read in this section has impacted you the most?

Why would you say that is?

In what ways do you feel lacking in freedom in your personal life?

What contributes to this?

If you could be free of one habit by the end of this book, which one would it be?

Chapter 2
The Roots of Addiction

"Fear and love are enemies. They come from two opposing
kingdoms. Fear comes from the devil, who would like
nothing more than to keep you permanently disconnected
and isolated. Love comes from God, who is always working
to heal and restore your connection with Him and other
people and bring you into healthy, life-giving relationships."
–Danny Silk

I began to pray for you as I was writing this section. I so want
you to come to a deep understanding of how God sees you
and how He views the problems that you have. I believe that
you can be totally free from the things that have always held
you from moving forward. But first, you may need to look
back a little.

A couple of years ago we travelled around part of Ireland
with my youngest brother and his wife. I was very struck by a
quote we saw on the outside of the *The Garrick Bar*, a pub on
Montgomery Street in Belfast. It said,

"A nation that keeps one eye on the past is wise. A nation
that keeps two eyes on the past is blind."

Not all recovery is forward looking. We may need to face
our past and deal with *why* we began the habits we can't
now break.

I pray that as you look back over your own past, God helps you to gain wisdom from it and not blindness.

This is a prayer that David prayed in Psalm 19:12-14. You might want to pray it too, before you read on.

"But who can discern their own errors?
Forgive my hidden faults.
Keep your servant also from willful sins;
may they not rule over me.
Then I will be blameless,
innocent of great transgression.
May these words of my mouth and this meditation of my heart
be pleasing in your sight,
Lord, my Rock and my Redeemer."

If we are honest, most of us have got deep-rooted discomfort that easily triggers and brings our addictive patterns to the surface. I believe that if we can recognise this and treat this (with the help of God,) we can learn to see those patterns coming and stop them from taking control.

Many addicts see things in black and white. They set themselves punishing and unrealistic targets. They say things like:

I will never gamble online again.

I will never eat another chocolate bar.

I will never set foot in a pub.

But of course, they then fail. They fall hard and start acting out all their behaviours again. This is because they say these things without reference to God or others and they try to help themselves *in isolation*.

Before we become Christians, the Bible tells us that we are all slaves to sin (see Romans 6:20). And until we are set free by Jesus we will remain enslaved. But our salvation gives us more than the joy of heaven, it gives us freedom and power on earth! It is this enabling resurrection power that helps us to say "yes" to Christ and "no" to the things that lead to our disquiet and dismay. Crucially, saying "yes" to Jesus also means we gain family members – Christian brothers and sisters who can help us move from our old life to our new one.

But we need to understand that it's not as easy as "just saying no". Saying no requires us understanding the roots of our problems. It also needs us to say "yes" to other healthy distractions or habits.

Think about it like this. If I am to have a beautiful garden, it is not enough to simply weed and clear a patch of earth and hope for the best. Why? Because weeds like nothing more than empty space! No. If I want a stunning garden, I must deliberately sow a number of new plants in the patch. Then I should cover the ground with some kind of mulch to stop weeds coming. The most effective weed treatment isn't to kill the weeds when they arrive, or wait until they get really unmanageable before tackling them, but to stop them having room to grow in the first place. We talk about habits we can cultivate to prevent re-growth of addictions later in the book. For now, lets examine some of the main roots of our addictions and how they can take over.

Isolation

The more I have studied, the more I have begun to believe that the opposite of addiction isn't simply just sobriety or restraint. It is something MORE than just *not doing the thing we feel compelled to do*. Which is what I used to believe. I now think that the polar opposite of addiction is actually *the freedom to be in loving relationship and connection with others*.

Galatians 5:13-14 (TLB) says:

"For, dear brothers, you have been given freedom: not freedom to do wrong, but freedom to love and serve each other. For the whole Law can be summed up in this one command: 'Love others as you love yourself.'"

In other words, our freedom isn't just for us. Our freedom is meant to exist in relationship, service and cooperation with others. (I talk about the serving suggestions for our lives more in my book *In Security – living a confident life*).

Let me explain more about what I mean by this in the context of addiction. I warn you, if you are an animal lover, you aren't going to like hearing about this first experiment! But it is a very useful springboard for us to consider.

A groups of scientists led by a professor of psychology in Vancouver named Bruce Alexander, undertook (what we might now consider cruel) sets of experiments with rats in the 1970s. Individual rats were locked in a cage alone and given a bottle of water and a bottle of water laced with morphine. They were then studied to see whether or not they would become addicted to the drugged water. All of them became compulsive drinkers of the drug and died.

Some time later, Alexander wondered what would happen if they changed the environment for the rats. They built something the scientists called "Rat Park". On his website, Alexander describes this facility as a "...very large plywood box on the floor of my addiction laboratory at Simon Fraser University. The box was fitted out to serve as a happy home and playground for groups of rats."

The box had painted walls, it was clean and had toys for the rats to play with. These rats were also offered the same drinks: water and another bottle laced with morphine. Alexander said, "My colleagues and I found that rats that lived together in this approximation of a natural environment had much less appetite for morphine than rats housed in solitary confinement in the tiny metal cages that were standard in those days."

He concluded that addiction isn't just about the chemical hooks that make a body dependent. It was something more complex and emotional. This discovery challenged the view that addiction is just a moral failing in society caused by materialistic party animals. It also disputed the belief that addiction is merely a chemical disease, taking place in an ambushed brain. Alexander started to wonder if addiction was more of an *adaptation*, an absence of purpose and connection. He began to wonder this because the rats that lived happy and fulfilled lives did not seem to *need* the drug.

There is a growing amount of evidence that suggests the same is true for people. In other words, addiction comes about more because of where we find ourselves than what we find ourselves going through. Journalist Johann Hari spent a number of years researching addiction in an attempt to personally understand and help those in his immediate family who were drug users.

The problem, he argues, in his highly compelling TED talk, is that we "punish" and criminalise addicts across the globe. We shame them and take them away from society. Having spoken to experts such as Alexander, Hari now believes that the exact opposite treatment is what would be helpful. He cites the country of Portugal as an interesting example.

For the last 15 years Portugal has had a controversial drugs policy that is markedly different to the guiding principles of the rest of the world. In 2001 the Portuguese decriminalised the use of all drugs. According to an article in *The Independent* (6th June 2015), "Portugal decided to treat possession and use of small quantities of these drugs as a public health issue, not a criminal one. The drugs were still illegal, of course. But now getting caught with them meant a small fine and maybe a referral to a treatment program —

not jail time and a criminal record."

The results of this policy have been utterly extraordinary. The Multidisciplinary Association for Psychedelic Studies (MAPS) cites that levels of drug use fell below the European average, HIV infections amongst addicts were significantly lower, and, despite fears of the opposite, the programme reduced crime, homicide and suicides.

So how did Portugal begin to treat its addicts? There were still residential rehabs and talking therapies offered, but these were not in prisons and isolating institutions. The programme began to give addicts different ways to reconnect with society. Government money was deployed towards job creation and micro-loans for apprenticeship-style work. The idea was to create a meaningful reason for people to get well and do something worthwhile as part of the community. And it worked. It reduced the power and stronghold of addiction.

I think this is *astounding evidence* that we are made for relationship and healed from dependency and addiction in community with others. When we are denied social interaction, taken away from society, our drivers for reform or self-discipline won't become strengthened, quite the reverse.

We all need to feel connected and bonded with God and with those around us. If we can't feel that, we will try and make connections with something else – anything else to numb the pain. But, as Brené Brown points out, the trouble with numbing pain is that it also numbs everything else too. We can't "selectively numb" anything. Numbing pain will also mean numbing joy, peace, courage and hope.

Reconnecting and bonding with others is perhaps the most therapeutic and healing change that could be offered for those trapped in the isolation of dependency.

How are you doing?

How do you feel about what you have just read?

Do you feel that the problems you have began in, or are made worse by, acute loneliness or isolation?

How do you think the Holy Spirit might be challenging you about that?

What could you do this week to put yourself in a place of community rather than loneliness?

Pain

Many therapists would agree that the root of most addiction is some kind of unresolved emotional trauma or pain. This may be extreme – for example, in the form of bullying, abuse, grief and loss – or milder, such as worry, insecurity or comparison. We dip ourselves or dive headlong into addictive behaviours because we can't bear to be present in the messy reality of our lives.

I don't think many of us do this consciously. I don't believe that I realised I was overeating to help myself feel better about having been sexually abused. I just found myself doing it, day in and day out. It was only years later, when I was at university and someone leant me a book on coping with pain after abuse that I started to see that my unhealthy patterns had had such a dark beginning. Each page I read felt as though someone was reading my personal diary. Things that I just thought were "me" and the way I operated, were in fact coping mechanisms for things I was trying to hide or process. It was an emotionally difficult discovery, but one I am so grateful for. It began a journey of healing in me that God is still taking me through.

Many addictions are birthed in a time of pain or crisis. As we said in Chapter 1, we humans go to great lengths to avoid pain, and will try lots of different things to anaesthetise ourselves from it. Consumerism, alcohol, junk food, entertainment, prescription pills, sex, and all manner of things are readily available to us as ways to avoid pain or hide from our problems. Our addictions are a way of diverting and comforting ourselves.

When traumas like these are not dealt with at source they can leave behind a mixture of painful, unprocessed emotional baggage. These feelings won't sit silently, but start to try and work their way out of us. Our emotions are always "in motion". They move us! But when we don't allow them to be brought into the open and healed, they will express themselves as "symptoms". They might move us to start some negative habits.

So, in me this looked like:

- Various attention-seeking behaviours – such as wearing loud, amusing clothes to get noticed, or doing outrageous things for a dare.
- Punishing personal rituals with food. Starving myself one day. Binge eating the next.
- Setting inconsistent and unreachable rules for myself.
- Constant self-deprecation out loud and in my head.
- Locking myself away from people and feeling afraid of contact.
- Or burning myself out, spending all my time with others.
- Poor self-care. Neglecting my teeth (I didn't go to a dentist for 9 years), hair and other bodily needs. Not getting the right food, exercise or sleep.
- Working too hard or not working at all.
- Lying or exaggerating to impress others.

- Flirting with men but then pulling away as soon as they were interested in me.
- Not being vulnerable with others or trusting some people too readily and telling them too much.

What a mess I was! I shuddered and then cried just now as I wrote that list of some of my behaviours. I can't think how I ever had any friends! But somehow God surrounded me with loving, kind and patient people who made sure I didn't hide myself away too much. And slowly, but surely, I have let those habits and behaviours go. More than this I have *replaced* them.

Your issues may be very different to mine. Obviously painful experiences can vary in their intensity and their consequences. Perhaps your addiction is rooted in the fact that one of your parents died when you were young, or in a relationship going wrong or in a bad situation at work. Another person may have depression caused by a sense of abandonment or fear and this has lead to your unhealthy habits or dependency.

Speaker and writer Beth Moore says:

"I am convinced now that virtually every destructive behavior and addiction I battled off and on for years was rooted in my insecurity."

I can't speak for other recovered people, of course, but the primary source of all my strength has been in the birth and growth of my personal prayer life. I'm not talking about going to prayer meetings or conferences about prayer – great though they are. I am talking about gentle hours alone with the Lord, wrestling for my peace, searching for answers and finding direction and security in Him. Before we moved to Manchester a number of years ago, I had to spend a great deal of time shut away in my little prayer room in the evenings, sitting with God and working through some deep issues that had clouded my life. It was very hard, very necessary and very healing.

But it isn't just in prayer that we find recovery.

In the book of James we read these words: *"Confess your sins to each other and pray for one another, that you may be healed."* (James 5:16 NIV)

Let me ask you a pertinent question.

When was the last time you did this?

When was the last time you sat with someone you love and trust and told them some of the areas in which you find yourself slipping up? When did you last openly acknowledge your wrongdoing?

It is very possible that I never willingly confessed a single sin out loud to another person until I was around the age 15. I think I had years and years when that just wasn't my personal practice. I have grown slightly better at it over the years, but I still don't find it easy. But I can tell you that it has been a significant key to my healing.

May I suggest to you that one of the reasons you might be struggling is because you don't confess anything to anyone? You keep your real, genuine self, locked away. You deny people seeing the authentic you, just in case they reject you. I used to do this too.

The Bible teaches us that healing from any addictive tendency isn't just found in the presence of Jesus, but in the people He has called to Himself. So much of what we lack is found in others. Forgiveness comes after confession.

I notice that if I run away from prayer or vulnerability with others, my balance can be skewed and it is much easier to develop secret habits again that are caused and characterised by my fears or failure.

I have learnt that I am loveable and worthy of love. Therefore, I am not as afraid to share parts of myself with my close friends that are messy or difficult. And you know what? Living this way gets easier. I recently had to share a pretty grim thing about myself with two of the girls I pray with. I knew I wouldn't get anywhere if I hid it. So I just told them. It was SUCH a blessing. Vulnerability like this produces real change. Not just in us, but in others around us too. It gives others permission to be genuine back. Plus, it actually brings healing.

Look what Paul says in Ephesians 5:18-19 (TLB) about drunkenness:

"Don't drink too much wine, for many evils lie along that path; be filled instead with the Holy Spirit and controlled by him. Talk with each other much about the Lord, quoting psalms and hymns and singing sacred songs, making music in your hearts to the Lord."

Did you notice that part of his solution to addiction was being filled by the Holy spirit *and* talking, worshipping and creating with others? When we are living a life of raw Christian community, vulnerable sobriety will become much easier.

Blame

We can all be guilty of playing the blame game. Brené Brown describes blame as a "way to discharge pain". We can accurately think that the things that happened to us are not our fault. We don't want to carry them, so we throw their weight onto someone else.

It isn't your fault that your Dad abused you. It isn't your fault that your Mum drank alcohol when you were in the womb and now you are an alcoholic too. It isn't your fault that you were taken into care. BUT, what you choose to DO about your problems now IS your responsibility. I know some people who have been damaged in the past who choose to continue to carry that bitterness and rage around with them. You meet them, you meet their anger. You chat to them and you hear some of the ways in which they are still hurting and enraged.

A year ago I was boarding the Statton Island Ferry in New York. A man got on wearing a T-shirt that pictured 9/11. The slogan said, *"Never forget. Never forgive"*.

Now I don't know the atrocities that man witnessed, or how many colleagues he lost that day, but I do know what he is still choosing to *carry*.

I hope I am different. I hope that when you meet me, you won't meet all the people who have hurt me or the result of their actions. Why? Because I have chosen to forgive those people and let God deal with them. It's not my job to bring justice, closure or repentance. That is up to the Lord. My job is to do what only I can do.

The Lord's prayer is very helpful here. It says, *"Forgive us our sins, for we also forgive everyone who sins against us"* (Luke 11:4 NIV).

Notice the word EVERYONE. It doesn't say, "Forgive those you love, or forgive those you find easy to forgive." It also doesn't say, "Forgive those who say sorry to you." We have to be those who forgive anyone and everyone. God knows that unforgiveness is like a cancer of the heart. It begins to eat away and destroy our peace. If we forgive others, our slate is clean and God can work His wonderful forgiveness in us. Our authority before Him comes from our humility in front of Him.

Forgiveness may need to be an ongoing thing. Occasionally I find myself floored by an emotion as I have a flashback to the past. This happened recently as I was brought face-to-face with a man who had once hurt me as a child.

My forgiveness had to "re-boot". I had to feel it and mean it all over again. I wasn't going to let him or that situation have power over me. I knew I had already won my peace about that. So I walked away from that encounter with no bitterness, condemnation or fear. I only felt compassion. For him, but also for myself.

You see, another hugely important part of us breaking the power of addictions and hurts is to learn how to forgive *ourselves.* I know for me that it has sometimes been much easier to forgive others for hurting me than to forgive myself for *letting* them. But I have had to learn to be kind to myself here. I have had to acknowledge that there have been times where I have been unwise or broken in the way I have treated others or allowed myself to be treated. But I have come to the peaceful and scriptural conclusion that God understands me and loves me without conditions! He knows all the cracks and creases of my life. He loves me through them and in spite of them.

Mark 11:25-26 (AMP) says: *"Whenever you stand praying, if you have anything against anyone, forgive him [drop the issue, let it go], so that your Father who is in heaven will also forgive you your transgressions and wrongdoings [against Him and others]."*

It took me a while to read that passage and realise that I wasn't including *myself* in it. I was thinking about others who I had a grudge against, not realising that I was bearing grudges against myself!

This version of the verse says I had to, "Drop the issue. Let it go". I think I have slowly done that. I have let myself off the hook.

Have you?

How are you doing?

Our friend Anthony who is the leader of the group of churches we are part of, is fond of talking about the fact that we have RESPONSE ABILITY. In other words we are able to respond to the things God needs us to.

How is God wanting you to respond to these words about forgiveness?

Are there people you need to forgive today?

Or should your forgiveness be even closer to home? Should you be looking at your own heart and forgiving yourself for the things you have begrudged in YOURSELF for so long?

You might say to me, "Ems, you don't know what I have gone through. You don't know how hard it's been. It's too difficult for me to forgive others. And as for myself ... I don't know where to start!"

Let me encourage you with a promise from the Bible. Deuteronomy 30:11-14 (AMP) says:

"For this commandment which I am commanding you today is not too difficult for you, nor is it out of reach. It is not [a secret hidden] in heaven, that you should say, 'Who will go up to heaven for us and bring it to us, so that we may hear it and obey it?' Nor is it beyond the sea, that you should say, 'Who will cross the sea for us and bring it to us, so that we may hear it and obey it?' But the word is very near you, in your mouth and in your heart, so that you may obey it."

I don't think forgiveness IS too difficult for you. I think it is very near you. I believe that carrying the burden of bitterness, malice and unforgiveness is MUCH harder. It is also never going to bring you peace or prosperity of heart.

The same power that raised Jesus from the dead is alive in YOU. You can do it! You can let go. You can be free of both blame and unforgiveness. Why carry it around any longer?

Shame

For years I felt dirty. I felt used and unclean. I had a deep shame that manifested in all kinds of ways. This is not surprising. Shame is a wound to the soul. It shows up in the way we feel and in what we think and say. Shame makes us feel "less" than others. Its ugly lies tell us we are flawed, defective and simply not good enough. It appears in our language: "I can never be what I hoped I would be..." Shame tells us that we can never fit in or feel part of any community.

Associated feelings might be extreme embarrassment, fear, anger, worthlessness or uselessness. We might also not want to "bother" people, tell them how we really are, or include them deeply in our lives.

Shame can also have physical symptoms. It can make us feel weak and ill, cause us to stammer or shake. It can make us bow our heads and avert our eyes from others. It can affect the way we look. I once knew a lady who was so weighed down by shame that it began to actually bend her spine. Shame seems to affect our whole being. Why?

Because it reminds of our dark secrets.

The story goes that the writer Arthur Conan Doyle sent letters to five close friends reading simply, "We are discovered. Flee now!" to see how they would react. Apparently, one of the friends actually disappeared and never came back. He obviously had something he desperately needed to hide!

The truth is, we all have things we are ashamed of. We also all have situations that have made us feel shame. One way to start addressing any deep emotions we may feel is to look at them slowly, piece by piece. We may need some help to start to examine the issues, actions, and people who trigger our shame.

Let me share with you a very preciously painful evening when God broke into my shame.

Deep breath. Here we go.

Jon and I had been married for 3 years. We were really desperate for a baby, but after my abuse I was left with a condition which made sexual intimacy impossible. We had gone for professional relationship counselling and been told by the cousellor that our marriage would probably collapse. Jon was told he was "masking his anger" about what had happened to me and that he would one day regret his decision to marry me. Let's just say, it wasn't the best year of our lives!

One evening, on a crowded train coming home from a meeting, we decided to ask for some prayer from an elder at our church. So, the lovely Jenny and Bill came over. We had not told them what we wanted to pray about. I was embarrassed and not really that ready to open up.

Jenny said she didn't know why they were there, but that her Bible reading that day (11th November 2003, Remembrance Day) had struck her as being relevant for me. She then read me the following words from *Daily Light*.

You were washed, you were sanctified, you were justified.
"The blood of Jesus his Son cleanses us from all sin. – Upon him was the chastisement that brought us peace, and with his stripes we are healed. – Christ loved the church and gave himself up for her, that he might sanctify her, having cleansed her by the washing of water with the word, so that he might present the church to himself in splendour, without spot or wrinkle or any such thing, that she might be holy and without blemish. – "It was granted her to clothe herself with fine linen, bright and pure"—for the fine linen is the righteous deeds of the saints. – Let us draw near with a true heart in full assurance of faith, with our hearts sprinkled clean from an evil conscience and our bodies washed with pure water.

Who shall bring any charge against God's elect? It is God who justifies. – Blessed is the one whose transgression is forgiven ... Blessed is the man against whom the Lord counts no iniquity, and in whose spirit there is no deceit."

(These verses are from the following passages 1 Corinthians 6:11; 1 John 1:7; Isaiah 53:5; Ephesians 5:25-27; Revelation 19:8; Hebrews 10:22; Romans 8:33; Psalm 32:1; Psalm 32:2)

Jenny had no idea that I was struggling with shame. I had no idea either. But this set of passages spoke right into the heart of the issues I was facing! It was such a beautiful night, as two godly people told me that I had nothing to feel ashamed of any longer.

Then Bill told me that he felt that I would be a "biological mother of children"! That phrase rang round and round my head with loud bells on. We hadn't even TOLD them what we wanted prayer for yet!

Two weeks later I naturally conceived our first child, who we called Samuel, which means "God heard". *How* I conceived is a real miracle ... but that's for another book!

Whatever the roots of your addiction or your habits are, NOTHING is too difficult for the Lord. Whether you are locked in despair, hopelessness, lack of joy, trauma or any kind of affliction, you *can* be freed. My experience has been just as it says in Psalm 56:9-13 (GNT):

"The day I call to you,
my enemies will be turned back.
I know this: God is on my side—
the Lord, whose promises I praise.
In him I trust, and I will not be afraid.
What can a mere human being do to me?
O God, I will offer you what I have promised;
I will give you my offering of thanksgiving,
because you have rescued me from death
and kept me from defeat.

And so I walk in the presence of God,
in the light that shines on the living."

God is able to rescue you and keep you from defeat. The question is, will you let Him?

Chapter 3
Knowing Real Freedom

"I'm not afraid of the devil. The devil can handle me – he's got judo I never heard of. But he can't handle the One to whom I'm joined; he can't handle the One to whom I'm united; he can't handle the One whose nature dwells in my nature."
–A.W. Tozer

What is freedom?

I believe that God's freedom is possible for everyone. And I don't say that in a naïve, bumper sticker, T-shirt slogan kind of way. I say it because I have met a woman in prison who murdered her daughter and told her she could be set free and watched her sob as we prayed. I say it because time and time again I have seen utterly broken people become whole and healed. I say it because God has said it over me.

But I want to explain what I mean by *freedom*. I am not talking about the kind of recklessness that allows us to do anything we like at any time. That kind of selfishness has never been part of God's plan. He knows this kind of autonomy would cause damage to us, and to others.

Do you remember in the Garden of Eden, God said to Adam and Eve, *"You may freely eat the fruit of every tree in the garden – except the tree of the knowledge of good and evil. If you eat its fruit, you are sure to die."* (Genesis 2:16: NLT)

God knows that not everything we want is good for us. He knew that eating fruit from the tree of knowledge would put up a barrier between us and Himself. And He was right wasn't He? The minute that first couple ate the fruit, they understood the nature of evil. They realised that they were capable of hurting God and each other. In a very real sense, death came into the garden.

In our society we are told, "If it feels good, do it!" But God's mentality is different. He says, "If it is good, do it." Our feelings aren't always a good indicator of right and wrong, especially when it comes to our habits. If we only use our feelings, we can often be led astray, can't we?

But is true freedom really possible for someone who would describe themselves as dependent or addicted?

New Creations

A few months back, I had the privilege of speaking at a small breakfast meeting in Manchester city centre. I got chatting to a wonderful lady before the event and asked her how she had come to know Jesus.

Without flinching she said, "Through my AA (Alcoholics Anonymous) meetings some 20 years ago."

I was fascinated and asked her more.

She told me that through the 12 steps that AA members practice, she had come to know the voice of Jesus and had begun to listen to Him. (You can find a copy of the 12 Steps in Appendix A at the back of the book).

She spent 6 years with those people at the meetings, learning from the others there. This gave her a great foundation for her faith and her recovery.

She told me that she MET Christ there, but it was only when she LET Christ into her whole life, and LET GO of her old ways of thinking that permanent change began.

"Do you mind if I ask you another question?" I asked. "Is

it your experience that 'once you are an alcoholic, you will always be an alcoholic?' I have heard so many people say that."

She smiled. "No!" she said, firmly, but gently. "I believe that the old has gone and the new has come. Jesus has made me new!"

The fruit of her life and the fruit of her lips told me this was true. I held her hand and told her how happy I was for her! Tears welled up in my eyes. Another person living the way God really intended!

This was a woman walking in real, genuine freedom and joy. She had learnt not to touch the tree of alcoholism that was so badly damaging for her, but was totally free to walk in the rest of the garden of God's love for her.

2 Corinthians 5:17 (NIV) says, *"Therefore, if anyone is in Christ, the new creation has come: The old has gone, the new is here!"*

I believe that each of us has a kind of personal tree of knowledge – something that we find it hard not to "eat from" or indulge in. When we do succumb to the temptations of that particular fruit we can experience great distance between ourselves and others, as well as detachment from the Lord. We are made to feel shame, guilt, powerlessness and loss of hope.

But I don't believe we need to stay there.

A Salvation Army Officer was once asked by a homeless man to sum up the Bible in one word. He thought for a while before saying, "Resurrection".

I love that truth. For me, the saying, "once an addict, always an addict" is simply not accurate. Why? *Because the story of God in us, is all about redemption, restoration and resurrection.* It is about dying and then being raised up. Resurrection is about new life!

This is also my own experience.

I was once addicted to making myself sick with a toothbrush.

Now I am not.

I was once addicted to bread.

Now I am not.

I was once obsessed with weighing myself every day.

Now I am not.

I was once addicted to being busy.

Now I am not.

I have interviewed a number of people for this book (you can read their stories later). All of them have told me the same thing: Jesus has set them free! He may have used a secular recovery programme to help them in their thinking, or to start them off, but HE has authored and will finish the work.

What I am learning from the dear people I am meeting is that recovery groups and rehabs can offer to REFORM us, and can do a very good job of that, but it is only in Jesus that we see our lives truly TRANSFORMED. Being transformed isn't about being mended and put back together. It's not about finding some kind of spiritual superglue and filling in the cracks. It's about being made a totally new creation.

I have seen this kind of transforming power first hand. Years ago I knew a very miserable person. He was unkind, unhappy and often unwilling to be part of his family. But when he became a Christian there was an enormous physical, spiritual and emotional change. It was as though someone had pumped new life and joy into his veins! He looked, sounded and behaved totally differently, overnight. His face looked renewed. The scowl was gone. The sarcasm was no more. It was truly one of the most wonderful miracles I have ever seen. This person continues to be one of the most loving, selfless and kind men you could ever hope to meet. He was utterly transformed. And we can be too!

As children of God we have the wonderful opportunity of

change every morning. We are being made more like Jesus and into God's likeness with every sunrise. His mercies are new every day. (See 2 Corinthians 3:18, Lamentations 3:22-23)

The best the world can offer is to put us back as we were before; to help us to stop a certain behaviour or tendency. Heaven offers us *so much more*. Heaven puts us forward. *It re-imagines us*. In many ways, relationship with Jesus turns our world the "right-way-up", showing us what we are really capable of.

Robert Frost wrote that, "freedom lies in being bold." There has never been a bolder claim than the one Jesus makes over our lives. Only He gives us that brand new life of total transformation from darkness into light.

You may have picked up this book because you want to be a "habit breaker" and I applaud you for that desire. But you may not have realised that GOD is actually the real habit breaker. I named the book after Him, not you. I have learnt that I can't achieve any lasting and purposeful freedom or recovery without Him. Only He can break into our addiction cycles and call a halt to the behaviour that makes us fail. Would you like to know that kind of power over your own life?

How are you doing?

I know this is a lot to take in. Especially if you have been struggling with your issues for a while, or if you have been told you will always have them.

How does my assertion that you *can* be free from your addiction or dependency or habit make you feel?

What are you using to back that feeling up?

Have a look at this verse and ask yourself if Jesus could have been talking about you when he said it.

"I am the gate. If anyone enters through Me, he will be saved. He will come in and go out and find pasture. The thief comes only to steal and kill and destroy. I have come that they may life and have it in all its fullness. I am the good shepherd. The good shepherd lays down His life for the sheep. (John 10:9-11 Berean Study Bible)

Jesus describes himself here as "the gate". In what ways do you need Jesus to open or shut some doors in your life?

What does the word "pasture" mean for you here? What pastures would you like to find in your future?

In what ways has the enemy been trying to use your habits to "steal, kill and destroy" what God has for you?

What are you going to do about it?

What would life "in all its fullness" look like to you?

So if the kind of freedom we have been talking about *is* possible for those of us who suffer with addictions (and I believe it is) what routes can we take to get there?

First we need to understand some of the barriers to that freedom.

That's dope

Some of us with addictive tendencies or dependencies will feel a sense of freedom from time to time. We may even feel as though we have "totally cracked it", but that might not be long lasting. We may find ourselves falling, all over again. This is because we are in a cycle.

Part of us learning to deal with our issues is understanding what happens to us each time we "fail". We need to realise that we are weak, that anything we indulge, feed, grow or deliberately sow will take hold in our lives. So let's look at how addiction can do that.

I need to do a bit more science chat with you again ... are you ready?!

Think about how you feel when something great happens in your life. Maybe you get a fabulous new job or you pass an important exam. You feel wonderful. Pleasure floods your brain. You feel a kind of natural high. This creates an appetite that drives you to seek more pleasure. So you try to find other ways to succeed and feel good about yourself. This is normal human experience.

But, if you start using fake methods to create dopamine, the brain physically starts changing. Let me explain. Say you start to take an addictive drug, for example. At first you will feel a real high of pleasure. But because of the unnatural flood of neurotransmitters, the neurons may start to *lower* the number of receptors or even *make less* dopamine in your brain. In other words, you won't feel as good for as long. There is less dopamine in your brain, so guess what? You will feel the need to up the dose of the drug to create more. Are you with me?

The more you act in this way, the more your brain responds by making less dopamine. The result of this is that dopamine's ability to activate all your pleasure senses is made continually weaker. You will start to feel lifeless, low and depressed. Life without that drug can seem utterly devoid of joy and hope. Now you will feel as though you need to use the drug in really heavy doses just to feel *anything* and get your dopamine levels up to a normal level.

So you then attempt higher and higher doses to feel an ever decreasing and shorter high, with a longer and more painful low. Constantly grabbing for something that will never truly satisfy you, you become tolerant of these higher levels of drugs. You use more to get you feeling good again. As you do this, more of your brain starts to change. The more you do something, the more your brain will respond to support that activity or circumstance. Scientists say that neurons that "fire together wire together".

It is why when some people try to come off drugs they become alcoholics instead, or pick up some other form of addictive behaviour. The neural pathways of dependency are built and ready to roll. Traffic will naturally flow on a road that is strong enough to carry it. One bad habit simply gets replaced by another one.

The changes in the brain caused by addiction of any kind are powerful drivers for people to look for ways to use substances, or forms of their habit, compulsively. In spite of the many negative consequences that come with such issues, like losing friends, family problems, stealing, lying, running out of money or other physical, mental and emotional needs, the substance/habit has them hooked.

If our addiction is severe we may start to fail in some of our duties at home or work. We may also experience physical harm, social problems and failed attempts to stop.

This is the sad and ugly pattern of addiction.

Unlocking the cage
I have known for some time that I have an addictive personality.

I can get obsessive about certain things for a while. Like Toad of Toad Hall in *The Wind in the Willows*, I can experience "fads" in my life in all sorts of areas – unless I am extremely careful. I have learnt to spot my little crazes and try to nip them in the bud.

I think this personality type was hidden from me for years in order to keep me locked into negative patterns of thinking. However, in recent years God has shown me more of what I am truly like and given me keys to set me free from those compulsive behaviours.

These kinds of characteristics can seem harmless, and even fun, but behind them is something rather sinister. For example, we may not realise that we are addicted to "appearing as though we have it all together". But that is an addiction. It is a mindset that is wrong. We are made for connection. As the body of Christ we are designed to NEED each other and function less successfully apart.

We may think that we need those new trainers, that new teapot, or scarf, or coat, but we probably don't. It is because we want to shop, to feel better, to distract ourselves and to forget something painful or annoying for a while.

This is how dangerous kinds of addictions form – because we stop being accountable and real and vulnerable with others (and ourselves) in the tiny but meaningful things.

So we find ourselves in debt, or gaining weight, or secretly smoking, or telling ourselves we will give up online bingo soon, or having a fantasy about another man's wife, or clicking on websites that are harmful to our holiness … the list goes on and on.

I heard just today about a man who became a severe alcoholic. He would take the day off work and drink neat bottles of vodka. He hid them in the rabbit cage in the garden. One day, his wife, who had no idea how bad things had got, told him she was going to clean out the rabbit. He went berserk, shouting at her and making up all sorts of rubbish to stop her going to the cage. But there, in all the spare straw were dozens of bottles. Apparently the marriage didn't last that long after that.

This man didn't want to face his problems. In fact he preserved them IN A CAGE. He locked them in. He hid them away. He couldn't give up his addiction because it was so precious to him. It meant life to him. Even though it was actually bringing him death.

We must face our problems if we are going to see any change in our hearts and lives.

The RE-cycle

One morning as I was praying, God showed me, in the clearest way possible, the way my mind functions when it comes to my weaknesses. When I feel low I:

- Relapse
- Regret
- Recriminate
- Repeat

This is the pattern my mind and heart can follow when I am tempted.

I RELAPSE. I do something I do not want to do and do not like doing. Perhaps it is shouting at my child rather than being patient with him. Perhaps it is eating something I know will make me feel ill.

It will be something different for us all.

The dictionary defines relapsing as "to fall back gradually". One definition actually uses the word "backslide". To regress after partial recovery is so easy to do. Why? Because it is almost imperceptible at first isn't it?

We slide back (not run back, or walk back, but slide) into

our former state.

This makes us REGRET our behaviour. We despise ourselves and feel sorry and sad. Often this makes us feel a sense of self-RECRIMINATION.

Did you know that the worst enemy you will ever have is yourself? I can promise you I am right on that. You are the only person who treats you so harshly. You are the only one who calls you those names and who is so down about who you are. The enemy does not need to attack some of us at all because we are so good at doing it all by ourselves!

What happens when we feel this bad about ourselves is that we REPEAT the behaviour. Why not? We have failed, haven't we? We may as well fail again and again and again. We deserve to fail because we are failures. This is the lie of what we can say over ourselves.

One of my friends was addicted to Porn. He hated that about himself but he couldn't stop because his self-hatred was so strong every time he did it. He had no self-love or self-belief that he would ever be free of the RE-cycle. He knew that once he felt weak and was tempted, he would enter this cycle of thought again…

RE-lapse

RE-gret

RE-criminate

RE-peat

What God showed me today is the power of ONE letter.
If you replace the letter "A" from the word REPEAT with the letter "N", what are you left with?

The old-fashioned word REPENT.

What does it mean?

You may know one meaning "to turn around", but did you also know that in Latin, the word repent comes from the verb REPENS which means to *creep forward*? Not slide back again, but move slowly ahead.

I think this is utterly brilliant.

Repentance doesn't mean everything is easy and you make leaps and bounds and are instantly healed, whole and holy, but it means you deliberately move away from the things that are weighing you down and holding you back.

I found this little download from God incredibly enlightening for my own understanding of me. I hope it helps you in your thinking about YOU too.

To further aid us in our journey, it might be helpful to look at what psychologists call the "cycle of addiction".

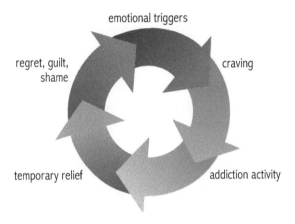

The addiction cycle may help you understand why you sometimes feel very different about your issue.

Let's say, for example, that you are a gambler. This is briefly what your addictive cycle might look like.

1. Emotional triggers. Something happens to make you want what you call "a flutter". Perhaps you feel upset, or angry. Maybe you feel excited and happy. Triggers are different for each person. You "listen" to your trigger and tune into it. You allow it room to grow.

2. Craving. Then you start to crave a gambling experience.

You think of how good you feel when you win. You think of the excitement of the bet. In this phase you don't think about the negatives. You just focus on the pleasure gambling gives you. You talk yourself into it. You excuse any doubts. You believe you deserve this "little pleasure". Your brain is bombarded with both excuses and plausible reasons why this will be ok for you.

3. Activity. You make a decision to gamble. You plan your route to your gambling experience. This may also include covering your tracks so that others don't know what you are doing. You bet, gamble or play a game. You may win or lose. The thrill is part of the pleasure.

4. Temporary relief. You feel a sense of enjoyment or comfort from the experience. You may get a feeling of satisfaction and relief. But it won't last. It will be painfully short-lived.

5. Regret, guilt shame. In this phase you feel overwhelmed by a familiar but unwelcome pattern of shame and guilt about what you have done. You think of all the people you have let down and the waste of money. Maybe you have burned through an amount of cash you needed for something else? You worry about how you will cope without it. You are ashamed about your habit and feel helpless. You may be anxious in case people find out. You may try other ways of stopping that happening.

6. Emotional trigger. You believe you are in a hopeless situation. You think you are a failure. You look back at what you've done and wonder how it got this bad. These feelings make you feel a deep lack of being understood and can make you feel unworthy of love. This may be an emotional trigger to start you off on your cycle all over again.

Do you see how easy it is to get lost in that pattern? Can you recognise any of your own behaviours there?

In order for us to leave our own cycles of addiction behind, there are two things we need to do:

1. ADMIT we have a problem
2. ADDRESS the problem and get support

Let's look at how we can admit our problem first.

So many of us choose to deny or decry that we have any problems or bad habits at all. Because it is so downright awkward and embarrassing to have to face some of the things we struggle with, we pretend those things aren't there or we try to minimise their impact in our lives. We hide our fears and failures; we keep things in the dark and hope no one finds out. The trouble is, constantly burying things under the carpet is eventually going to create such a bump, it will trip us up!

Our church leader, Anthony Delaney, used to be a police officer in Manchester. He told us the true story of someone who tried to evade arrest. The man was clearly drunk. Anthony started to ask him some questions. The man stood amongst the crowd, trying to blend in. When questioned, he just protested in a loud voice, "I am an innocent *stybander!*"

Proverbs 28:13 says, *"Whoever conceals their sins does not prosper, but the one who confesses and renounces them finds mercy."*

You can't hide sin for long without it having consequences. Why? Because it is so powerful.

1 Corinthians 15:55 (Weymouth New Testament translation) says, *"Now sin is the sting of death, and sin derives its power from the Law."*

Our sin has a way of catching us out (see Numbers 32:23). It wants to trip us up. Let me explain a little more. You see, sin has no life in it. Everything connected with sin has the stench of death attached. This is because sin was designed by the enemy to put a wedge between us and God. Simply put, I think this means that everything we do wrong has the capacity to damage us and others. These things create distance, fear, shame, regret and a feeling of unworthiness that can make us turn from God, back into ourselves.

James 1:14-16 in the NLT says, *"Temptation comes from our own desires ... These desires give birth to sinful actions. And when sin is allowed to grow, it gives birth to death. So don't be misled, my dear brothers and sisters."*

The phrase "sin ... gives birth to death" used here is a horribly vivid one isn't it? But it is true. Nothing that comes from giving in to temptation will ever bear good fruit. Failing leaves a bitter taste in the mouth and the heart doesn't it? Doing something "again" that we have tried not to do, will make us feel beaten and low.

Feeling unloved and unworthy can make it harder to repent and leave us more likely to *repeat* our failures. Then more shame is heaped upon us by our lack of progress and change. People in this position start to voice feelings like:

God can't love me!

I'm not worthy of His attention.

I can't be forgiven because I keep sinning.

I am worthless!

I might as well give up trying.

C.S. Lewis understood this battle well. He said, "There is no neutral ground in the universe; every square inch, every split second, is claimed by God and counter-claimed by Satan." This battle can leave us feeling exhausted and overwhelmed.

A kick when you're down

This is what the enemy will capitalise on. He will try to blindside us into making wrong choices when we feel downtrodden, by feeding us with the kind of statements that ensnare us even

further. We find ourselves thinking thoughts like:
One won't hurt.
I will never be free, so what's the point of trying.
If no one knows, it's not that bad.
It's only hurting me.
I will start again tomorrow.
I don't really have a problem.
I can stop whenever I like.
I deserve this. I've had a hard day.
I've eaten one, I need to finish them all now.
It will be too hard for me to give up.

The devil will also try and take our eyes off all the good things that God has promised us in the future and just make us focus on NOW.
I need a smoke *now*.
I need a drink *now*.
I need cake *now*.
I need sex *now*.

He doesn't allow us to think about the rewards we might get later. For example:
- I will be healthier when I am not reliant on drugs.
- I will feel better when I am not as overweight.
- I will sleep better when I have cared for my body by exercising.
- I will have more money to spend when I'm free of gambling.
- My family will be more peaceful if I stop acting out of anxiety.
- I will be more content when I am not obsessed by this situation.

There are so many rewards to be had in waiting for the *right time* for the *right things* (I look at this in Chapter 4). But many of us never play those wise words in our heads and try to shut down any of those long-term, more sensible feelings.

The devil and our fleshly thoughts will dangle temptations into our minds. Mood-altering substances, Internet gaming or porn, or somebody else's husband or wife, could all be lures wafted in front of us. The enemy of our souls lies to us and tells us these things won't really hurt us; that we deserve to be happy. He will show us all the areas where we are not satisfied. He will make us *want*.

One thing that the Psalmist David says about God in Psalm 23 is this:

*"The Lord is my shepherd, I shall **not want**."*

This phrase, "I shall not want" is one of the most beautiful truths we can ever hold on to. It is a wonderful thing to be content.

One of our old family friends wrote a song based on this psalm. It began,

"Because the Lord is my shepherd, I have everything I need..." This is the truth. All other assertions are merely plausible lies.

How are you doing?

Be honest with me and with yourself for a minute.

Are there things in your life right now that you are allowing, excusing or hiding? Are there behaviours that you have just "let slide" because of your circumstances or situation?

Have you said, "When I'm not grieving any more, I

will stop overeating." Or, "When my divorce has come through, I won't drink as much on my own."

Are there behaviours you feel ashamed of and would be mortified if someone "found you" doing them?

Please don't wait until that happens to sort yourself out. Don't wait for a rabbit cage moment! There is another way to handle the problems you have.

I pray that the Holy Spirit speaks to you right now in this moment and that He highlights anything that you need to face and deal with.

One of the reasons I am writing these words right now is because I do not want you to be misled. I don't want you to live a life that is characterised by constantly succumbing to temptation. Because that will make you feel rubbish. Permanently. I don't want you to have to live in a cycle of repeated failure. I want you to be an overcomer! I am sure you do too. Deep down, none of us want to be weak-willed or foolish. We don't want to live a life where sin is allowed to grow.

I feel very strongly right now that some of you are raging mad as you're reading. As I am writing, I can feel that someone out there just wants to throw this book in the fire and hit the bottle! You feel so angry and hurt by my words because they are jangling your last nerve! They are jumping on the vulnerabilities that you have been hiding for so long and you just want me to shut my mouth.

I see you.

And so does God.

But I am not going to shut my mouth – or close the laptop I'm writing on. Because you need to hear the voice of God to you today. You don't have to die an addict. AND you don't have to live like one either.

You have a life that is worth living. You can be *set free*.

I am praying for you in this moment, that you would neither give in, nor give up, but that you would choose to see your life as worth more than the price you currently pay for your pleasures.

Take a breath and decide to work with me. OK?

So, are you ready to truly admit your problems?

If you are, here are some ways you might find useful to do that. They are not necessarily in the order you might feel is right for you. Do pray about that and see what you feel led to do first.

1. Tell yourself how you feel and what you are doing. This might sound a bit bonkers. You might think that you are VERY well aware of your problems. But I know that for years I didn't truly face what I was doing, how I was eating and what my issues actually were. I had never sat down and asked myself why I behaved the way I did and what the root causes might be. Nor had I thought about when they had begun and what triggered them. By asking yourself some key questions and facing up to what your behaviours are, you can start to think about how you can get the best help and support.

In Appendix B at the back of the book I have written you a list of questions you can use to get you started. I guess this goes without saying, but I will say it anyway ... the more honest you are with yourself at this stage the better. Hiding what you are really doing, feeling or thinking is counter-productive and will slow your progress and healing.

Paul Tripp said, "No one is more influential in your life than you are because no one talks to you more than you do." So it's important to tell yourself the whole truth and not half of it.

2. Tell God. This might sound crazy too. Surely God already knows everything about me? Well, yes He does. But there is a big difference between Him *knowing* and you sharing it with Him. There is something powerfully healing about unburdening ourselves with open, out-loud confession.

Often when we are in trouble of some kind, we feel trapped and enclosed by our problems, don't we? Psalm 188:5 (NIV) says, *"When hard pressed, I cried to the Lord; he brought me into a spacious place."* We all need a spacious place in which to think and move forward. Maybe we need to cry out to the Lord?

You might say, "But Ems, I don't know what to say. I feel so ashamed!" The Bible reminds us that, *"...the Spirit helps us in our weakness. We do not know what we ought to pray for, but the Spirit himself intercedes for us through wordless groans"* (Romans 8:26). The truth is that if we tell God what we have done, He acts in the light of what He has done. He knows how to deal with it. Because He already has. We can't surprise or disappoint Him or change how He feels about us.

Remember that God promises to be near to all those who call on Him, especially when they do it honestly, "in truth" (see Psalm 145:18). Telling Him where you have messed up and how you feel will bring you closer to Him. Psalm 16:7 describes God as a counsellor, saying that He can even help to restore us in our dreams. It says, *"I will bless the Lord who has counselled me; indeed, my mind instructs me in the night."* No human therapist could ever offer us free round-the-clock care like this!

3. Search Scripture. I love the Bible. I feel as though whenever I need an answer to anything I am facing, somewhere in its pages will be words of comfort, challenge or encouragement.

Because God breathes through the words, and they are "living and active", they get to the heart of our problems. God's word probes us, prods us and produces fruit in us. Whatever your issue, let me encourage you to find and declare scriptures over your life at this time. Appendix C contains a list of some Bible promises you might want to speak out. But please don't JUST rely on those words. Dig for your own treasure and let God show you just how amazing He is at knowing your needs and answering your questions through Scripture.

4. Tell someone who loves you. I know how hard this is to do. But I do believe it is key to your healing. The first time I told my Jon that I had been abused as a child and that this had left me with some strange behaviours, beliefs and hangups, I was nearly sick with fear. I knew that I loved him and wanted him to love me. I knew he wanted to marry me, but at this point he didn't know my whole background. I was terrified that understanding I was damaged and messed up would make him want to run like the wind! I was worried that he might see me as "soiled" in some way.

He was only just 20 when I told him – really very young to have to handle such a painful and complex amount of disclosure. It took me around 6 hours to get all the ugliness out. It was the most horrendous conversation I have ever had. But I can't tell you how amazingly he handled it. God has made Jon to have a very steady nature. He is not easily dismayed, angered or liable to form grudges. His heart is incredibly soft and wise. Telling him gave me hope. It was an amazing foundation for our marriage and helped me start to believe I was loveable and even lovely. It has also helped me to deal with my addictions and know that he understands where they come from and why they rear their heads at certain times for me.

Telling someone you love that you don't like or understand

part of yourself is a hard journey. It is unpleasant to open ourselves up like this. But I don't know any other way to intimacy, forgiveness, healing, unity and grace. If you choose the right person, someone who loves you and loves God, someone who is mature and wise in their outlook and demonstrates being slow to anger and abounding in love, you will find real positives. You see, the Bible tells us that this kind of person's prayers are authoritative and valuable. Talking to them and asking them to pray for you is part of your recovery process. Look at the second part of James 5:16:

"The prayer of a righteous person is powerful and effective."

I praise God that Jon's prayers for me have been this. They have helped to transform me and make me whole. Telling someone your issues may have the same deep impact on you.

Address the problem

So now that we know the extent of the problem, how do we get out from under the cycle of our addiction? In 1 John 1:8-9 (AMP) we read these comforting words:

"If we say we have no sin [refusing to admit that we are sinners], we delude ourselves and the truth is not in us. [His word does not live in our hearts]. If we [freely] admit that we have sinned and confess our sins, He is faithful and just [true to His own nature and promises], and will forgive our sins and cleanse us continually from all unrighteousness [our wrongdoing, everything not in conformity with His will and purpose]."

I love these verses because they contain the answer to my heart's needs! If I admit I have done wrong and bring it into the light, God does what I can't do! He forgives me. But there is more to it than this.

God's laundry

A few weeks ago my eldest son came home from rugby, utterly filthy. His muddied knees and shirt made for a sorry sight. Everything he was wearing was wet and clung to him in the grey drizzle of the early evening. He looked pale, exhausted and fragile. I took a good look at him and tried to work out which need to meet first. I didn't know whether to feed him, hug him or wash him.

"How do you feel darling?" I asked.

"Dirty!" said Sam.

His overriding need wasn't food, nor was it a cuddle because he didn't want to be touched. He felt dirty. He wanted to be clean.

I ran upstairs to start the shower whilst he peeled off his sullied kit.

Because He is faithful, God knows my biggest need. Because He is just, He can do something about my need. God knows I am unclean, and He chooses to *continually cleanse* me from all I do wrong. When I'm dirty, he bathes me. He doesn't just let me stay dirty.

Malachi 3 talks about God being like "launderer's soap". God understands that addictions make us feel unclean. They cause us to hide away and keep things hidden in darkness. Once we have admitted our issues to Him, ourselves and others, there are ways in which we can begin to tackle those problems and seek out permanent change.

Here are some ways you can start to address your addictive behaviours. At various times in my adult life I have done all of these things. I can recommend that they work, are helpful and practical.

1. Seek professional help. However helpful it is to tell a spouse or pastor or friend, there will be times when talking to a trained professional is the right next step for us. This is especially the case if our issues are complex and multi-layered. Proverbs 13:10 (ERV) tells us, *"Pride causes arguments, but those who listen to others are wise."* There is a list of helpful agencies you can access in Appendix D.

2. Join a support group. You may find it beneficial to be part of a group that aims to help those who need recovery. Some agencies now offer online support as well as course material. Local churches may run "Freedom in Christ" or recovery courses that you can access, too. You may find that some kind of residential rehabilitation programme is best for you, especially if you are suffering with a substance addiction. This helps tackle the initial task of withdrawal in a safe environment and helps to support you in lifestyle changes that will allow you to overcome your habit.

3. See your GP. Going to see your doctor means you can be told about free advice clinics or health professionals in your area. A mixture of talking therapies and medication may be offered to you. The NHS also has a brilliantly simple but helpful set of websites for people who are struggling with addiction and those caring for them. You will find these listed in Appendix D too.

4. Practice saying no. As we said in Chapter 1, we live in a world where saying "no" is made more difficult by 24-hour accessibility. If we simply start to practice the art and discipline of saying "no" to ourselves when we crave something, even if this is small, it can help make us feel more confident and in control. We learn that our desires and cravings pass. This is a very key step for overcoming any temptation we face.

5. Remove triggers. Take away things that cause you to

repeat your behaviour. I once knew a lovely girl who had a severe shopping habit. In the end she spent so much money that she was in debt to the tune of thousands of pounds. She was using store cards to purchase things and paying them off each month. But these left her huge bills to pay, plus the interest she was accruing. Once she had finally paid off her bills, we had to help her to destroy the cards so that she couldn't get herself into that kind of mess again.

What causes you to repeat your behaviour? If it is staying up until everyone else is in bed and being online, don't do that! If it is shopping when you are hungry, don't do that!

6. Talk to a financial expert. You may be all too aware that your habit is physically costly and that this has led to deeper financial insecurity and anxiety. Appendix D gives you information about contacting CAP (Christians Against Poverty) who help thousands of people access debt relief advice and services and rebuild their lives with Christian support.

Bible-inspired recovery

The Bible is so helpful about what we need to do in our weakness. I recently rediscovered this passage in Ephesians 5:10-14 (NLT) which I found so enlightening. This short scripture is a wonderful set of verses and gives us some brilliant principles we need for our recovery. It says:

"Carefully determine what pleases the Lord. Take no part in the worthless deeds of evil and darkness; instead, expose them. It is shameful even to talk about the things that ungodly people do in secret. But their evil intentions will be exposed when the light shines on them, for the light makes everything visible."

Lets go through, step by step and see what we learn:

1. "Carefully determine what pleases the Lord." Firstly, we need to find out what God wants from us and the things that make Him happy. This has taken me years in the area of my eating. I have had to study, pray, cry, laugh, talk to people, reverse my thinking, research, write, and rewrite my ideas. Reading the Bible, talking with wiser Christians, being part of an accountability group … all of those things can help us find out what pleases God in our lives.

2. "Take no part." Secondly, we need to choose to take no part in deeds that will displease Him. We need to make it hard for ourselves to fall. If our problem is cream cakes, we need to not go to the bakery. If our problem is gambling, we need to disable all those gambling apps from our devices.

3. "Worthless deeds." Thirdly, we need to look at our addictive actions as bringing no purpose, life, hope or fruit to our lives. Only when we see that they aren't adding anything to our days will we be willing to leave them behind.

A friend of mine was very sad when he was forced to give up his drinking. It felt like a personal death for him. It was. Drink had been a friend to him. Admittedly, a very bad one – but a friend, nonetheless. Repentance does sometimes lead to sorrow. Not because we have hurt others, but because we will be hurt by letting it go. But we need to focus on what the consequences of NOT doing this are. My friend knew that if he wanted to make his life work, he could not keep excessive drinking as part of it.

4. "Expose them." Talking about things that have been hidden makes them appear more manageable. Telling a trusted friend

or accountability partner what we have done is hard but, as we have already said, it's worth it. Bringing things out into the open is the only way to begin dealing with our addictions.

5. "Shameful even to talk." Some of us fall into the trap of talking about our problems all the time – almost glorifying the situation. It is important that we share with others, but our habits shouldn't always dominate every conversation. Don't gossip your issues to get attention or special treatment or seek to magnify them in any way. Looking for sympathy in this manner nearly always backfires and leaves us feeling hurt. Sometimes, talking about the problem, but not doing anything about it, can make it feel so much bigger. Decide now to keep your words about yourself and your addictions as positive as you can.

6. "Shine light." Continue to shine light on your life. Don't give up trying to work out what is going on and don't get tired of recovering. God's work in us is a lifelong commitment and He will never get weary of us.

Once we have admitted our problems and begun to address them, how do we stop falling back into old patterns again? Here are some simple things we can do to help ourselves.

Ways to prevent relapse
1. Avoid what triggers you most.
2. Make contact with new people who don't have the same problems as you, so your life feels more open to the possibilities of change.
3. Serve others. Find people who need something and offer it. Changing our perspectives can be a powerful driver for growth.
4. Only meet up with other recovering people if they support

your new habits, not if they endorse or stimulate your old addictions.

5. Change your activities. Find different ways to relax and unwind. Very often people get into drugs or addictions of other kinds to enjoy themselves. Find other healthy ways to seek and find pleasure.

6. Journal or write down all the benefits of your change. Reread them to avoid going down those routes again.

7. Plan ahead. For example, if you know you are going to a funeral and it will trigger emotions or put you in a situation that might make you vulnerable to relapse, agree certain rules for yourself in advance. For example, have someone come with you, or drive you there and back. Or make sure you meet up with someone a day afterwards to talk. If I am going to a party, I will text my recovery group beforehand to ask them to pray for me, so that I don't overeat or eat foods that harm me.

Nelson Mandela is quoted as saying:

"There is no easy walk to freedom anywhere and many of us will have to pass through the valley of the shadow of death again and again before we reach the mountaintop of our desires."

I really believe that we can achieve mountaintop freedom with the help of our Habit Breaker God, and that with Him all things are possible! We will see how some other people have reached the mountains and left their valleys later in the book.

For now, lets focus on how we can best help ourselves.

Chapter 4
Caring for Yourself

"It is not the critic who counts; not the man who points out how the strong man stumbles, or where the doer of deeds could have done them better. The credit belongs to the man who is actually in the arena, whose face is marred by dust and sweat and blood; who strives valiantly; who errs, who comes short again and again, because there is no effort without error and shortcoming; but who does actually strive to do the deeds; who knows great enthusiasms, the great devotions; who spends himself in a worthy cause; who at the best knows in the end the triumph of high achievement, and who at the worst, if he fails, at least fails while daring greatly, so that his place shall never be with those cold and timid souls who neither know victory nor defeat."
–Theodore Roosevelt

Leading yourself

A while ago I went on a retreat and was asking God about my leadership. I wanted Him to tell me some new things about my focus. But I was quite surprised as I was praying, because, rather than give me some keys for leading others, I heard Him say:

"The most important person I am asking you to lead in this season is yourself. At the moment you have swallowed the lie that your life is about leading others. Primarily this is not true."

I found this really challenging.

It was not what I had expected. At all.

I had to ask myself the question, "Am I easy to lead?" and "Do I lead myself well?" If I'm honest, the answer is that often I am high maintenance for myself to lead. I give me a hard time! I have high standards and don't always make the grade of my own ideals. Then I whine at myself for being so weak.

What about you?

Are you good at leading yourself?

Part of getting over any addiction is to understand yourself well and give yourself good patterns of thinking. This means leading yourself (especially when no one is looking!) and making sure you are led by other strong, godly leaders too. I realised that I am much better at submitting to the authority of others over me, than listening to or regulating myself. I had to ask God what self-leadership looked like. Over the next few weeks, God highlighted a number of ways in which I was malfunctioning in this area.

- I set myself improbable targets
- I didn't encourage myself when I was doing well
- I didn't give myself any slack if I was ill, tired or stressed
- My expectations were not always biblical
- I wasn't being consistent
- I did not use the standards on others that I used on myself

Does any of that sound familiar to you too?

If we are going to lead ourselves well we also need to learn to accept and love ourselves. I write about this a lot in my book, *In Security – living a confident life.* Some of us find this almost impossible. We have grown up being so awful to, and about, ourselves that it is hard to change this bad habit.

Yesterday I was talking to an older lady I know in the

playground. She spends half her year travelling the globe and was telling me about her latest escapade.

"Does it help you to leave your troubles behind?" I asked, smiling.

"Not at all. You take yourself wherever you go," she said. "I don't see it as a means of escaping myself at all. I do it to understand myself more."

I am glad my friend had worked this out.

Joyce Meyer talks about the fact that we must have the kind of love for ourselves that agrees with how God feels about us. If God loves me then I must love myself. This doesn't mean we have to love everything we do, but we do need to choose to accept ourselves because God accepts us. We can't reject what God sees as worthy.

How does that last sentence make you feel?

Have you constantly rejected yourself, even though God sees you as worthy and honoured in His sight? It may be that you need to ask Him to help you change in this area.

Create a good environment for change

Martin Luther King Jr is quoted to have said, "The Christian gospel is a two-way road. On the one hand, it seeks to change the souls of men, and thereby unite them with God; on the other hand, it seeks to change the environmental conditions of men so the soul will have a chance after it is changed."

Many of us need help to create a good environment for ourselves to thrive, grow, change and leave old ways behind. What that is like for each of us will be different, but it might have some common threads. Hopefully, the rest of this chapter will help you work out what your best environment for change looks like.

Don't focus on speed

A few weeks ago I watched a fascinating short film about

a businessman who described how, when he started his little company, he needed to provide "enough runway" for success. I loved that phrase and I found it so helpful. The truth is we won't "fly" straight away. Most of the recovery process is slow. We may grind to a halt for a while, or continue to crawl into position for what seems like ages. Planning for this stage of growth by visualising enough runway ahead is so useful. One day we will fly! But until then we must keep moving forwards one tiny, faltering step at a time.

One day, when I first started running, I was mortified to find myself overtaken by an elderly Indian lady walking in a restrictive Sari! To say that I am an unhurried runner is an understatement. I may well be slower than a geriatric tortoise (with rickets), but I lap everyone on the couch or still in bed! I might not be Paula Radcliffe, but at least I am putting one of my tiny feet in front of the other. For me it's not about winning a race or beating my time. It's about me not standing still, doing nothing.

You may take months or years to get over your addictions. Or it may be literally overnight. I don't know. But I do know that you can move away from them, one small step, or one giant leap, at a time.

Helping yourself towards recovery

"Do not be conformed"

Romans 12:2 (ESV) says, *"Do not be conformed to this world, but be transformed by the renewal of your mind, that by testing you may discern what is the will of God, what is good and acceptable and perfect."*

At the beginning of any personal journey we need to stop copying others and work out what we, ourselves, are in need of. Not being "conformed to the world" means just that – not always doing what others expect of you or falling into the trap of having to react and behave like them.

Secondly, we need to be transformed – not by botox or therapy or rehab – but by the *renewing of our minds*. Then, and only then, can we understand what God wants for us and from us.

My recent UCB notes by Bob and Debby Gass in *The Word for Today* had something fascinating to say that links to this thinking. They said,

"Researchers identified more than a hundred identical twins that had been separated at birth. They were raised in various cultures, religions, and locations. By comparing their similarities and their differences it became clear that as much as 70 per cent of their personality was inherited. Their DNA determined such qualities as creativity, wisdom, loving-kindness, vigour, longevity, intelligence, and even the joy of living. Consider the 'Jim twins' who were separated until they were thirty-nine years old. Both married women named Linda, owned dogs named Toy, suffered from migraine headaches, chain-smoked, liked beer, drove Chevys, and served as sheriff's deputies. Their personalities and attitudes were virtual carbon copies."

Having identical twins myself, I am always captivated by this kind of research. But what do studies like this show us? Is it that we are just like puppets, playing out a predetermined role, as though reading lines in a pre-written play? Are we really incapable of free will or choice? I don't think so, at all. My twins have the same DNA, but they are so different in so many areas. I think their personalities and characters are massively distinct, even if their genes are not.

Unlike any other creature on the planet, humans are capable of both rational thought and independent action. When our minds are renewed by the Lord, we won't have to act on every physical urge, or every addictive thought, in spite of our genetics or our nurture. Our heredity may lead us in a certain direction, but our impulses can be brought under God's control. This is where the new birth of the Christian comes in. God gives us a new nature and also the power to have victory and dominion over our old one.

One of my friends, Sophie, told me this amazing story about her own past recently. She said,

"Myself and my sister weren't raised in a Christian family, but we attended the local church youth group. When I was 16, my Dad suddenly died of a heart attack. After his funeral, there were lots of family arguments which resulted in me leaving home. I last saw my sister when I was 21. I decided to do my own thing and turned my back on faith and church and got used to the fact that I had no family now. Five years ago, I recommitted my life back to God after meeting my church leader at work and being invited on an Alpha course. A few weeks ago, after 12 years of not seeing my sister, she contacted me. We met up for coffee. I asked her what she was up to. She said, 'I'm a student pastor at a church.' I was shocked. I told her that I have just moved to a church plant and we are on a mission to reach students at our local university campus! It was then that I knew God had had His hand on our lives all that time. I just didn't know it."

I love this so much! Even though these sisters were not brought up with faith, and had a really difficult time growing up, God clearly had a wonderful plan for their lives.

1 John 5:4-5 in The Message says, *"Every God-begotten person conquers the world's ways. The conquering power that brings the world to its knees is our faith. The person who wins out over the world's ways is simply the one who believes Jesus is the Son of God."*

Even if your family life was a disaster, or you have since had major trauma, there is HOPE for you. You are not defined by your mistakes or your mishaps or how well you did at school. You are not what your medical prescription or your diagnosis says you are. If Christ is in you then you are an infinite number of hopeful and wonderful possibilities, all headed towards healing and joy!

As I just finished writing those words I looked out of the window. In the sky above me were a flock of migrating birds. They suddenly formed a perfect arrow in the sky! I think it was a sign, just for you. God is on your case today. He is moving you from one state to another. Keep believing for your breakthrough!

Be a person of praise

I am still learning so much about the power of praise in my life. There have been times recently when things have gone wrong for us as a family and I have felt a challenge in my heart to "sing anyway". Just a couple of weeks back, our daughter opened our passenger car door violently into the brand new car next to us (costing over £400 to mend). The day after that, the bath water wouldn't drain away and the plumber who came to sort it plunged water so hard that the waste pipe detached and leaked water all over the floor. This then came through the kitchen ceiling and blew all the lights. An electrician had to be called and all the light fittings needed to be changed. It was literally one thing after another!

But I remembered what I'd heard speaker Graham Cooke say at a conference once. He reminded us that every curse and every problem in life had an opposite promise in the spiritual realm. Deuteronomy 23:5 says that God turns intended curses into blessings because He loves us. So I claimed those opposites and found myself laughing about our string of expensive mishaps and claiming God's mercies to help us through them.

In Acts 16:25 we are told that, *"About midnight Paul and Silas were praying and singing hymns to God, and the prisoners were listening to them."*

These amazing men of faith managed to keep praising God even when they were thrown in prison! And the result of this was that God sent an earthquake of such magnitude that it shook the foundations of the jail. All the doors of the cells opened, and the chains on the prisoners fell off! This is what can happen to our lives and our addictions when we praise God, right in the midst of our captivity.

Fear has no choice but to depart when you praise. Anxiety is sent running. Worship becomes a weapon! It is the last thing the enemy expects to come out of our mouths. It puts him off guard. He thinks we will whine and winge. If we worship instead, that will be a life-changing, life-impacting decision – not just for us, but for those around us. The only time I want to be someone with my head down is when I am saying AMEN!

Incidentally, I thought you'd like to know that two days after all those things happened in our home, we had an unexpectedly large royalty payment for a show Jon wrote four years ago. It more than covered those bills! Do you think God is teaching me to respond to my worries with worship?

Have you been with someone going through a crisis and felt empowered by how they are responding? That is the power of the worship-filled life.

Nothing inspires me to praise more than someone raising their voice and their hands in worship, or digging deep into their pockets for others, when I know that life has become impossibly hard for them. Praising and choosing to live generously like this is something God loves.

What does the Bible say?

Psalm 34:17 tells us that, *"When the righteous cry for help, the Lord hears and delivers them out of all their troubles."*

He may not do it the way we hope, or think we need. And He rarely, if ever, does it in the timeframe we pray for. But God is always, always doing us good. He will use our problems to do us good. He will use our hardships to do us good. He will use our illnesses to do us good. He will use our griefs to do us good. He doesn't need goodness to do us good. He is a God who can make beauty from ashes and joy from heaviness. (I talk about this a lot in my book *Good Grief – Living through loss* available from my website, www.emshancock.com)

Don't complain

A lot of the time we just grumble about having to struggle with our issues. This can easily turn into self pity as we say things like, "I am fat because my dad was an over-eater." Or we say, "I am a drunk because my marriage broke down." Or, "I am type 2 because I lost my job."

We say, "Nothing can change for me. Things just go wrong in my life. It has always been like this." We justify our lifestyle or behaviour with excuse after excuse. Self pity like this is a warped form of hero worship. It makes us out to be the "hard-done-by-guy" all the time. It blames others for the problem and also expects them to be the solution. This is not good for change. Grouchy, disagreeable language that talks about the size of the issue doesn't help us. In fact, it allows even more discouragement to come and play on our minds and take over our hearts. It won't change anything because it doesn't contain anything positive or godly.

I used to look at shiny, fresh-faced people around me tucking into a kale, quinoa and beetroot salad with what looked like enjoyment ... go home and wade through a multi-pack of crisps. I wondered how they could ever really like what they were eating. I felt rubbish that I struggled. I whined about my weight. But this kind of feeling had no power to change anything for me.

The "why me?" attitude, coupled with the refusal to change won't get us much further than the sofa, will it?

Philippians 2:13-15 (NIV) says, *"For it is God who works*

*in you to will and to act on behalf of His good pleasure. Do
everything without complaining or arguing, so that you may
be blameless and pure, children of God without fault in a
crooked and perverse generation, in which you shine as lights
in the world."*

I want to shine as a light in the world. I don't want to be
dimmed or darkened because of the habits I pursue.

Psalm 42:5 says, *"Why are you cast down, O my soul, and
why are you in turmoil within me? Hope in God; for I shall
again praise him, my salvation."*

Understand the "fakeness" of pleasure

As humans we are fairly unique, in that we can be lulled
into enjoying fake pleasures. For example a Yale-based
psychologist named Paul Bloom recalled a famous
experiment amongst wine drinkers by scientists at Stanford
and Cal Tech. He is quoted as saying:

"Half the people are told they're drinking cheap plonk, the
other half are told they're drinking something out of a $100-
$150 bottle," Bloom said. "It tastes better to them, if they
THINK they're drinking from an expensive bottle. And it turns
out that if they think they're drinking expensive wine, parts of
the brain that are associated with pleasure and reward light
up like a Christmas tree."

It is alarming that we can be so easily fooled. We can be
fobbed off into thinking that we have the real thing or that we
are enjoying something we are not. But the Bible isn't fooled
at all. It warns us that the enemy masquerades as an angel
of light (see 2 Corinthians 11:14). He will tempt us towards
things that "look pleasurable" but are actually harmful.

In what ways do you find yourself easily influenced by the
opinions of others? Does this ever rob you of pleasure? Or
maybe your attitudes sour other people's experiences?

As Christians we need to set the tone for the atmosphere

around us. We are the temperature and the thermostat. Does the way you live your life breathe life into others? Or do they see you coming and take a deep breath?!

Resources for recovery

Never before has there been so much help available for those of us who struggle. There are some wonderful online resources and books. For example, if you struggle with over-eating, over-exercising, food addiction, or any kind of eating disorder, you can listen to some of the amazing podcasts on the Overeaters Anonymous (OA) website. I have put some other suggestions for you to try in Appendix D at the back of the book. There is even a new Bible called the *Life Recovery Bible: leading readers to the source of recovery – God Himself* which contains amazing features to help people overcome all types of addictive behaviours.

One of the things I have had to learn is to set aside time to actually act on the things that have been given to me. It's no good knowing there are great resources out there if I don't take time to access them and process what I have learnt. So turn the TV off and get yourself sat in front of your computer. Watch a TED talk, or a sermon. Listen to a podcast. Read great books. But make sure that you give yourself time to think through the material you hear.

H.A.L.T

Alcoholics Anonymous and other therapeutic groups such as OA, use a helpful acronym that describes four physical conditions which, left untreated, can stop us in our tracks and leave us feeling vulnerable to some kind of relapse. The word H.A.L.T stands for:

Hungry
Angry

Lonely

Tired

Now, of course, these are common human experiences. We are likely to feel at least one of these things most days. This does not mean that we will relapse every day. But, this acronym is a useful self-help tool to remember in terms of what those things might trigger in us.

As we have already said, relapse will look different for each addict. It might look like excessive gambling, inappropriate sexual activity, TV binging, shopping, overwork or drug or alcohol abuse. It may also produce old belief systems that result in us feeling shame, guilt or condemnation.

1. Hunger obviously does not just mean a lack of food, although physical hunger can be a powerful trigger for some addicts. More than this though, many of us can be hungry for love, attention, comfort, friendship or conversation. It is so important that we have people around us who can help us to meet those emotional feelings in healthy ways.

One of my friends had a huge need for physical touch. As an older single lady, she missed companionship. She needed big old physical bear hugs. Not the namby pamby kind. The ones that squeeze the life into you! When she went to church, she could rack up about 30 hugs from different people of all ages in one morning. She was seen as a Grandma figure in her community and this delighted her.

We all need our emotional needs met in safe places and in safe ways. Perhaps you will find your emotional hungers met in a 12-Step recovery group. Or maybe, like my friend, you will discover this in your church, your family or in another group setting.

For years I tried to meet my emotional hungers with food. But I have learnt that the way in which I feel accepted and helped to deal with my deeper underlying "hungers" is by being in a loving and caring church community.

2. Anger is a little more tricky for us to talk about. The great news is that there is nothing wrong with us actually feeling angry. We know that Jesus got angry at times (see Mark 11:15). But what is more complex and challenging is the way in which we learn to express that feeling wisely and maturely.

One of the girls I used to mentor really struggled for the first few years of her marriage, because she had never seen her parents argue. So she had no mechanism for handling anger in her own relationship.

Constructively dealing with inner rage is something we do not model well in our society. Every sit-com, drama or soap has people screaming and shouting at each other. Plates fly! Doors slam! Relationships end. Cars screech off. Every newspaper is full of arguments and anger between countries, communities or individuals. Either we have see people fly off the handle at the slightest thing and be unpredictable and frightening, or we are shown volatile emotions being masked, hidden or squashed.

Neither is actually massively helpful for us to mimic is it? Unfortunately, sometimes the way we convey our anger takes hugely destructive forms. Our feelings can turn our anger against ourselves or towards others. We can lash out verbally or physically. Its forms can range from being critical and negative to actually physically violent or self-harming. Some anger builds up into deep resentment which, left unchecked, grows and festers within us.

I once knew a little girl who self-harmed in a bizarre way. When she was hurt or angry she took it out on herself by ripping up a painting she loved that she had done, or by deliberating messing up her room. The only person she was hurting was herself. But she didn't know any other way to release her emotions.

What if it is someone else who has hurt us? How should we act then? Matthew 18:15 says, *"If your brother sins against you, go and tell him his fault between you and him alone. If he hears you, you have gained your brother."*

John Bevere says that, "Many people apply this scripture verse in a different attitude from the one Jesus was intending. If they have been hurt, they will go and confront the offender in a spirit of revenge and anger. They use this verse as justification to condemn the one who has hurt them."

But Jesus does not want us to seek out a person who has hurt us in order to condemn them, but instead to seek reconciliation. We are meant to try to remove any barriers and seek to restore the relationship.

The Big Book of Alcoholics Anonymous suggests in step 4 that a person with resentment towards another should pray for that person. *Prayers From The Big Book (AA)* says,

"We asked God to help us show them the same tolerance, pity, and patience that we would cheerfully grant a sick friend. When a person offended, we said to ourselves, 'This is a sick man. How can I be helpful to him? God save me from being angry. Thy will be done.'"

In other words, they are asked to imagine every good thing that they would wish for themselves, heaped with compassion onto that person's life.

"If you have a resentment you want to be free of, if you will pray for the person or the thing that you resent, *you will be free.*

If you will ask in prayer for everything you want for yourself to be given to them, *you will be free.*

Ask for their health, their prosperity, their happiness, and *you will be free.*

Even when you don't really want it for them, and your prayers are only words and you don't mean it, go ahead and do it anyway. Do it every day for two weeks and you will find you have come to mean it and to want it for them, and you will realise that where you used to feel bitterness and resentment and hatred, you now feel compassionate understanding and love." (From an AA member's story, *Freedom from Bondage*).

I have found this a particularly useful tool when I have prayed for anyone struggling to forgive or let go of an old resentment. As we pray, God often enables us to see how this person has acted and why. Rather than focus on the build up of the anger, God shows us the needs of the other person. This can dissipate the resentment hugely. Unexpected resolutions to the conflict can then surface as new insights into the situation are given.

There are, of course, many other forms of anger that have destructive out-workings. When we become angry, there are some simple things we can do to "offload". Some people find it useful to take time out, to stop, breathe, and try to gain some control of their emotions. Others will find it helpful to talk out loud, or write a letter (as if to the person who has hurt them) to let out their emotions. The letter is not one that will be sent, but one that enables the angry person to become better connected with and express their own feelings. Others who suffer with anger, may need to do some kind of physical activity such as going for a walk, punching a cushion, or running, to let out the surge of negative emotional energy they feel.

The other day I was a little hurt by a particular circumstance. It left me feeling confused and angry. Rather than take this out on myself by over-eating (something I used to do without even thinking), I decided to go for a run. I ran further than I have run in months. I think the emotional energy of all I was feeling helped me to out-do myself! I came home with renewed energy and a creative solution to the feelings I was struggling with.

It is always important to try and work out where the

underlying cause of our anger stems from. If you have on-going problems with constructive expressions of your feelings, you may need a period of professional help. In order to understand more about rage and learn about where it comes from, I have found Joyce Meyer's audio teaching on how to handle and deal with anger very simple and helpful.

3. Lonely is the next trigger in the HALT acronym. Like those poor laboratory rats we mentioned in Chapter 2, loneliness leaves us feeling vulnerable to addiction, isolated or abandoned. Interestingly, loneliness is similar to hunger, in that the solution – being part of a loving community – is also the same. However, people who are lonely often struggle to be, or feel, part of a wider community life. They find it hard to reach out to others. This deep loneliness can have several causes, some stemming from childhood. Mental health problems such as depression can also lead to someone feeling unable to be around others easily.

Psalm 68:6 (NLT) gives us God's heart for lonely people. It says, *"God places the lonely in families; he sets the prisoners free and gives them joy."*

If you feel as though heightened feelings of loneliness have followed you for an extended period and you don't seem to be making progress to step out of those emotions, you may need to seek some prayer or counselling to look at the root causes. God wants you to be set free and given joy in exchange for your despair (see Isaiah 61).

4. Tired. We all have a tendency to ignore our tiredness at times. We keep going even when there are clear benefits from stopping or slowing down. Dr Wayne Scott Anderson MD, medical director of "Shape for Life" says, "Exhaustion has been linked to issues with appetite regulation, heart disease, increased inflammation and a 50 percent increase in your risk of viral infection." Extreme tiredness is a serious condition that endangers our wellbeing as well as that of others – especially if we drive or operate machinery while drained and exhausted. The solution to this is obviously to nap or sleep more. Lack of sleep can be caused by feelings of stress or overload from work or family situations. In some cases, sleep problems can be caused by underlying medical issues. If you are having trouble sleeping and this has been over a prolonged period, please go and see your GP.

How are you doing?

In what areas would you say you often feel hungry? Physically? Emotionally? Spiritually?

Not all hunger is bad for us.
What kinds of hunger do you think are positive in your life?

What areas of your hunger have a negative impact on you?

In what ways are you good at dealing with your anger?

How is anger sometimes a trigger for your addictive behaviours?

How does knowing that help you prepare yourself emotionally?

When we feel lonely we often reach for the wrong thing to soothe ourselves. Can you remember a time when you turned to a bad habit because of loneliness?

If you experienced that emotion again, what could you do instead?

How are you feeling having read the HALT material above?

Do you feel tired at the moment?

What is causing this?

What could you do to protect yourself from exhaustion over this next month?

Running on empty

One of the best talks I have ever heard is called "Dead leader running" (available on YouTube) by pastor Wayne Cordeiro who is founding pastor of New Hope Christian Fellowship in Honolulu, Hawaii. This talk helped me truly begin to understand how I operate when I am tired. I encourage every person I mentor and every couple we meet with to watch this talk and discuss it together. It is truly brilliant.

Wayne has also written a book called *Leading on Empty* which further explains his helpful and practical ideas. One of the things he recommends is working out what "drains" you and what "fills" you up again. If you can see patterns forming in your calendar where you know you will be drained, you put some kind of "filler" into your diary.

This is something that Jon and I find very helpful.

Caring for others

Are you looking after someone who suffers from addiction or dependency? Or are you a small group leader or pastoral worker in a church?

If so, this short section may help you.

Firstly, well done! You will know that caring for someone with addiction is hard. It can often feel frustrating, worrying, thankless work. But it is so worth it when we see those we love come into freedom.

Most of the ways in which we seek to care for others are problem centred. What I mean by that, is that we focus on the presenting issue that the person shows us – the addiction, the illness etc – and treat that first. Someone tells us they are struggling, so we pray into and about that struggle.

For example, say a lady called Chloe comes to see you. Chloe has addictive problems with alcohol and she's a heavy smoker. She doesn't get out much and tends to feel depressed much of the time. Where do you start with Chloe?

Problem-centred care is a way of looking at Chloe where we think of her as a "problem" person. We see people as "normal" if they are free from mental, physical or spiritual problems and function well in work and social settings. "Normal" people like this don't need much help or lengthy pastoral care. In this way, we see that pastoral care is only for people like Chloe – those whose life falls below these standards in some way. The aim of what we are trying to do is to restore those people to what we term a "normal" condition.

Going back to Chloe, we would say that our goal for her is to stop drinking and smoking and become a more active member of her church community.

I recently read a helpful article by Mike Jobling that really challenges this idea. He argues that the New Testament model of pastoral care is not problem-centred but goal-centred.

The goal of each of our lives as Christians is not to be "normal" but to be made more like Jesus. In other words we ALL need help! None of us has arrived at the destination. We are all on the journey. He suggests that we should not be focusing on our problems, but on our goal. We should not be saying to Chloe, "Let's sort out your problems" but, "How much are you like Jesus?" Paul sums this up well for us in Ephesians 4:13 (NIV):

"...until we all reach unity in the faith and in the knowledge of the Son of God and become mature, attaining to the whole measure of the fullness of Christ."

The aim of any care we show Chloe or anyone else in addiction, or indeed any other problem, needs to be to help them to *become more like Jesus*. In fact, this should be the goal of every prayer we pray for every person and for ourselves.

Are you spending hours with someone like Chloe who is locked into addiction, trying to restore them to some kind of normality? Could it be that this person's greatest need is not for that normality, but for your unconditional and loving acceptance? I think it is possible that sometimes our problem-centred approach to pastoral care, unwittingly gives people the message that we only care about them when they are needy. That they will lose this precious time with us once they are doing better. Perhaps this might make Chloe feel we will be less loving to her once she is restored? It might even prolong her emotional need to see us. She doesn't want to give up that intimate, cosy, supportive time with us. And why would she?

Our goal for ourselves and others should be that we reflect Jesus, and help others do that, not that we become more "normal" or like everyone else.

So maybe for the Chloe in your life, you can start to ask

Jesus what kinds of prayers you can be praying for her spiritual life that need dealing with, before looking with her at those addictions.

Show them what they look like

More than ever we rely on the Internet or self-help books to help us work out how we are feeling. The problem is that we can Google our problems and self-diagnose them without talking to anyone. This can be dangerous. If we are not careful we can under-play or over-dramatise our issues.

As people caring for addicts, we need to help those in our care to see what they really look like and what they really struggle with. I hope that some of the exercises and questions in this book will do that for those you are caring for.

During my research I discovered that a retail giant based in Birmingham in the UK is now taking down mirrors from its three largest malls in a bid to boost the confidence of female shoppers. A spokesperson said,

"We want to ensure that everyone feels comfortable and confident when trying on clothes, so that's why we're trialling banning the mirrors."

The idea that if we don't look at ourselves we will feel better about how we look is pretty crazy! Of course, the retailers are hoping for more impulse buying. They are relying on people buying something and not really knowing what it looks like until they get home. Many of us don't want to go through the hassle of taking something back … so it's a win for the marketing and the retailers. But is it a win for us?

I don't think so. Not knowing our problems will never help us feel better about ourselves long term.

We need each other to get a balance of what we look like. But sometimes we also need a good hard look in the mirror too.

How Jesus cared for Peter

I think we learn a great deal about how to care for others in addiction by looking at Jesus. Jesus showed us just how powerful it is to have an accountability partner to help to confront us, challenge us and comfort us when we are trying to recover. He demonstrated this beautiful relationship in the account from John 21 where He showed love and truth towards Peter without scorning him, or adding to his guilt and shame.

In many ways we see the life of the addict in Peter. The loud mouth, impetuous man who "just can't help himself". The one who argues with Jesus when it came to the washing of feet in John 13. The one who cuts off the ear of Malchus in John 18:10. Capable of great faith that leads him to walk on water (Matthew 14:28-31), he is a man of powerful opposites. It was his hands that had distributed miraculous food to five thousand hungry people (Matthew 14:19). It was he who had witnessed the glory of Moses and Elijah standing next to Jesus on the Mount of Transfiguration (Matthew 17:4). This was the brave, brash, Peter who said to Jesus, *"Even if I have to die with you ... I will never deny you!"* (Matthew 26:35 NLT).

But, as you may remember, Peter wasn't always faithful. In fact, the Bible tells us that he did publicly deny Jesus – not once, but three times. He laughed at the thought of even being associated with Him and when Jesus needed him, he ran away and wept bitterly (Luke 22:54-62).

Until this point, these men had been best friends. They had done everything together. They had had huge adventures. Bonding times. Deep, personal, life-changing conversations. But then a cock had crowed and with it, all of Peter's bravado had ebbed away.

Peter was in real need of recovering after his traumatic incident and had to undergo some genuine changes in his character. No one understood that more than Jesus.

Unlike many addicts after failure, we see Peter, to his credit, staying with the group of disciples – even after the pain of his denial (see John 21:1-3). This is important for his future and to help make sense of his past. He stays with people who know him, understand him and love him.

Then we see how Jesus Himself fills the role of the accountability partner for his faithless friend. Not only does he seek Peter out and feed him (see vv.4-14) but he also blesses him with a huge catch of fish, and shows compassion to him, before speaking to confront him.

Only after they finish eating does Jesus talk privately to Peter (v15-22). Jesus' words to Peter are really interesting here. This "reinstatement" as the Bible calls it, is such a precious transaction.

In v15 we see Jesus saying, "Do you love me more than these?"

Peter's reply is, "Yes, Lord, you know that I love you."

Jesus then says, "Feed my lambs."

So what is Jesus really talking about here? I think He is saying, "I give you authority to work for me again. I know that you have plenty to offer. I know that you are more than capable of bringing people up in my ways. I love you. I trust you." Wouldn't you love Jesus to say that to you?

Again we read that Jesus said, "Simon son of John, do you love me?"

He answered, "Yes, Lord, you know that I love you."

Jesus said, "Take care of my sheep."

The third time he said to him, "Simon son of John, do you love me?"

Peter was hurt because Jesus asked him the third time, "Do you love me?" He said, "Lord, you know all things; you know that I love you."

Jesus said, "Feed my sheep."

This repetition is important. Jesus is undoing the three denials with three opportunities to declare his love. Jesus is replacing lies with truth and darkness with light. He is exchanging sadness with joy. For the mentor, this is a wonderfully important skill.

As we said earlier, the goal of all of our lives isn't to be "normal" it is to be more like Jesus. Here we see the Lord giving Peter this simple instruction: *"Follow me!"* (21:19) We are called to do the same, to follow and to be like our Master.

In recovery from addiction, we are asked to honestly examine the past. Peter had to do this with Jesus. He had to face his pain and his shame, so that his ministry and his love for Jesus could continue to grow.

We know that Peter made a remarkable recovery from this incident and went on to be a strong, brave and bold disciple who preached to thousands and healed others (see Acts 2:14-22, Acts 3). Jesus even told him that the early Church would be built on him (Matthew 16:18).

Helping people to recover means we must be like Jesus ourselves and remind them of their priority to be like Him too.

What can we learn from Peter here?
- We need to have an honest view of ourselves.
- We need to stay with the group that tells us who we really are.
- We need to be willing to replace old patterns of thinking with new ones.
- We need to serve Jesus and others.
- We need to maintain intimacy with God.
- We need to believe that we are capable of being restored.
- We need to be willing to lead again once we are asked to.

What can we learn from Jesus here?

- He met the physical needs of Peter before he dealt with his problems.
- He didn't make Peter feel more anxious or guilty about what he had done.
- He was not shocked, angry or disgusted by Peter's behaviour.
- He was compassionate and godly in His actions.
- He didn't rake over the past or say, "I told you so."
- He allowed Peter to feel the full depth of His love.
- He reinstated and trusted His friend again.
- He spoke words of life and encouragement over him.

So what about you?

If you could chat to Jesus right now, what is it that your heart would say? Maybe you could write some words down now as a reminder of where you feel you are up to today.

Chapter 5
Habits to Cultivate

"Habit is overcome by habit."
—Thomas a Kempis

Resolutions

On the first of January each year, people around the world make determined, noble-sounding statements about how things will be different this time. As they scale the unlikely and dizzying reaches of their imaginations in compiling these lists, they may not realise that they are aiming to combat or cushion some of their deepest insecurities.

Each list will be personal, of course. Some may write in flowery tones about being healthier, looking more vigorous, repeating joyous thoughts out loud, achieving soul nourishing tasks, or drinking protein life juices, containing seeds and hemp.

Other dairies will boldly state in crisp, stark, no-nonsense bullet points something like,

• ONE macchiato per day
• Bi-weekly spinning class
• Leave work by 6pm
• NO cigarettes

In *Bridget Jones's Diary* by Helen Fielding we read this rather telling resolution:

"I will not ... Sulk about having no boyfriend, but develop inner poise and authority and sense of self as woman of substance, complete without boyfriend, as best way to obtain boyfriend."

Our promises to ourselves tell us a lot about what worries us, don't they? They show us how we see ourselves and give us a glimpse of what we feel others may think of us too. In short, they are a clear indication of our fears. And this might be the key to why we don't actually keep them.

Come on. Be honest. Who of you has made a list of New Year's resolutions that didn't even make the end of teatime on January 2nd? I know I have.

I never did learn sign language.

Or join a gospel choir.

Or do that floristry course at night school.

According to an ITV viewer's poll for 2016, the most common resolutions people make are to:

• Lose weight
• Take up a hobby
• Cut down on alcohol
• Get a better work/life balance
• Change their relationship status
• Stop smoking

Most of us can scan lists like that and know that we have made similar ones. We might have scrawled them on a notepad somewhere or kept them as the wallpaper of choice on our phones. Or, if you are anything like as stationery-obsessed as me, even purchased special paper for such a hallowed record.

But maybe, just maybe, you have given up making any kind of declarations or promising yourself any attempt at change, because you are fed up with the lack of genuine, lasting progress you make? Maybe you don't want to try anymore because you can't handle the disappointment of staying the same, or getting worse?

But ultimately this kind of attitude is the *burglar of joy*. Growth and change are ESSENTIAL if we are to become more like Jesus. Because of Him we ARE capable of massive, outlandish, audacious, crazy, miraculous, hard-won, disciplined, self-controlled and glorious change!

So why is it that very few of our best-laid plans ever seem to make it past those foggy, watery days of early February? Why is it that personal transformation is so tough? In the *Path to Happiness* St Nektarios of Aegina wrote:

"How mistaken are those people who seek happiness outside of themselves, in foreign lands and journeys, in riches and glory, in great possessions and pleasures, in diversions and vain things, which have a bitter end! ... Happiness is found within ourselves, and blessed is the man who has understood this. Happiness is a pure heart, for such a heart becomes the throne of God ... What can be lacking to them? Nothing, nothing at all! For they have the greatest good in their hearts: God Himself!"

I find this breathtakingly beautiful.

Maybe we are looking for happiness in the wrong place?

Maybe our problem is that we try and tackle too much too soon from a place of unworthiness or unhappiness? Maybe our lists are too long? Or too diverse? Or too impractical, or expensive, or just not what we actually NEED? Maybe our lists are not about why we want to change? Maybe they press the buttons of culpability, but not the buttons of challenge? Maybe they are not made in dialogue with the God who loves us and lives within us?

One of the most ugly things we may need to face is the guilt we feel about our bad habits and addictions. We feel guilty. Maybe not all the time, but certainly most of it. We feel guilty about not changing. The generations before us survived wars, depressions and political unrest. They endured harsh rationing and learnt how to make passable meals using nothing more than two parnips and a hair net. But we languish in our PJ's, struggling to find the energy to change channel!

We need to remember that guilt never built anything lasting. Guilt overwhelms us. It shames us, causes us anxiety and fear. It makes us curl up in a ball and want to hibernate, but it doesn't help us develop or change.

Guilt causes us to create the wrong lists and then feel so intensely crushed by the sheer weight of them that we don't know where to begin. So we turn away and self-medicate with a Sky box set and a double-layered box of Thornton's Continental instead.

Because we live in a fast-paced culture, we want our changes straight away. We want our weight lost through miracle diet pills, overnight. We want immediate fitness through boot camps, overnight. We want money, food, goods and services immediately, or overnight.

But what we don't want to do is INVEST in our own change over a long period.

Say we want to lose a few pounds and so that goes on the list of resolutions. We might start well and then, a few days in (or sadly sometimes, a few hours in), we find ourselves losing focus. Dietician Abigail Wilson, the chief executive of ISOShealth.com, says that on average the people she sees committing to new year diets only last a matter of weeks.

"These diets are just that, they are diets, but they are not behavioural change and do not last for very long. The diets you choose need to be able to fit within your lifestyle. They need to be something that is realistic. It's taken 10 years to get where you are with your weight, you're not going to be able to fix it in five weeks."

Wilson's advice is: "Choose to overcome one behavioural

change at a time and then move on, rather than making a whole lot of changes all at once."

ONE behavioural change. That doesn't sound like much does it? But it could be the difference for you between misery and joy.

Deep down we know the truth that if we lived less out of habit and more out of intent, life would really change. If we tackled something, ONE THING, until it was achieved, sorted and healed we would make massive progress. Imagine your worst habit obliterated from your life. For ever. How would that feel?

It would be amazing wouldn't it?

So what foundational principles can we cultivate that will help us build lives where we are healthier, happier and holier? I suggest five different broad brush strokes over the next few pages. I believe that if we concentrate on ONE of these things, our underlying habits WILL change. Remember, ONE behavioural change at a time is possible.

1. Intimacy with God – knowing who He is
2. Self-knowledge – knowing who you are
3. Self-control – knowing how to be disciplined
4. Balance – knowing how to tackle extremes
5. Staying power – sticking with recovery when things are hard

Intimacy with God

We might struggle to think how we can be intimate with someone we cannot physically see or touch, or share a meal with. But the Bible is clear that closeness to God is not just possible, but that it is foundational for a good life. Knowing who God is and how He feels about you will totally change how you do everything.

It is, as Steve Curtis Chapman once explained, the way in

which we hear the song God is singing "over all the noise" of our lives. Having said that, there is no easy Christian path for us to follow to help that to happen. God is a God of mystery and delight. He loves us looking for Him. He loves it when we search for comfort from Him and for relationship with Him, rather than in that e-cig or at the bottom of a bottle. But there is no fast track to getting to know Him; no speed dating app that will get us closer to Him. Instead, we are promised that if we will seek Him with all of our hearts, we will truly find Him (see Jeremiah 29:13).

To do something with all our hearts takes courage, conviction and determination. You can't accidentally love in that way, can you? Deuteronomy 6:5 tells us to, *"Love the Lord your God with all your heart, all your soul, and all your strength."* Like me, you may have heard that verse a thousand times. But have you ever thought about what it means for you and how you actually do that? What does that kind of love look like?

I guess for many of us we have to look at the way we love others to give us a glimpse of the way we can love God. If you ask me who I love, and how I love, I can speedily point to my husband and my children. I have no problem loving them with my whole heart. I am totally for them and I struggle not to go on about them the whole time! They are my priority in life and I adore them. In the same way we should love God with wholeheartedness and be ready to talk to Him and about Him all the time. We should not be ashamed of our love for Him and we should make being with Him the priority.

David understood this when he wrote in Psalm 27:4 (NIV), *"One thing I ask of the Lord, this only do I seek: that I may dwell in the house of the Lord all the days of my life, to gaze on the beauty of the Lord and to seek him in his temple."*

There will, of course, be times when we seek God out of true desperation, especially if we are struggling with relapse or illness. Life can be hard and there will be days when we will need His presence, His healing or His guidance. Other times we will come to Him out of sheer desire, hungry and thirsty for more of Him. But there will also be days when we seek Him in dryness and desert periods. These times of disciplined diligence are also precious.

It is often in those dry times that we find ourselves questioning God, but getting to know Him better too. I am so grateful that much of the Bible is written with this kind of inquiring language of God. Many of the Bible's characters say to Him:

Who are you?

Where are you?

What are you doing?

How long are you going to let this go on?

This encourages me!

We don't have to sit tight-lipped in front of God, hoping our questions and doubts won't explode out of us. We can voice them. We have God's permission.

Do you remember the story in the Bible where Jacob wrestles with God? (see Genesis 32). After this, God renames him, Israel.

Among the understandings of this new name are:

"One who wrestles with God" and also "one who is straight (direct or honest) with God".

I love this!

I love that God chooses to name one of His children the equivalent of, "Tell Me how you are. Tell Me how you feel. Tell Me what you're thinking!" God is not afraid of our questions and doubts. In fact, like in any healthy relationship, He wants us to voice those things to Him, not bottle them up.

In the AA movement it is interesting to note that the 11th step of the 12 steps to recovery method says, "(we) sought through prayer and meditation to improve our conscious contact with God as we understood Him, praying only for knowledge of His will for us and the power to carry that out."

It is through intimacy with God that we come to know more of His will for us and are given the strength we need to take action.

One thing that God wants from us is our genuine affection. He doesn't want us to make a fake show of our relationship with Him. In fact, in Amos 5:21 we see Him declaring,

"I hate all your show and pretense—the hypocrisy of your religious festivals and solemn assemblies."

Why did God say that? David knew this when he penned Psalm 51, where we read in verses 15-16:

"You do not desire a sacrifice, or I would offer one. You do not want a burnt offering. The sacrifice you desire is a broken spirit. You will not reject a broken and repentant heart, O God."

Intimacy with God brings us many things. One of the most beautiful is that our names are recorded in Heaven as those who love Him and think about how to please Him.

Malachi 3:16 (NLT) tells us,

"Then those who feared the Lord spoke with each other, and the Lord listened to what they said. In his presence, a scroll of remembrance was written to record the names of those who feared him and always thought about the honour of his name."

You might ask HOW you get to know God better? There are many wonderful ways to invest in your relationship with Him. I find that reading the Bible, listening to His voice, meeting with other Christians in church and smaller groups, reading great books and hearing inspiring talks help me.

How are you doing?

Do you feel you have real intimacy with God?
What could you do today to seek Him and develop a
closer relationship with Him?

You might like to pray this beautiful ancient prayer of
St Patrick known as "St Patrick's Breastplate".

I rise today
with the power of God to pilot me,
God's strength to sustain me,
God's wisdom to guide me,
God's eye to look ahead for me,
God's ear to hear me,
God's word to speak for me,
God's hand to protect me,
God's way before me,
God's shield to defend me,
God's host to deliver me,
from snares of devils,
from evil temptations,
from nature's failings,
from all who wish to harm me,
far or near,
alone and in a crowd.
Amen.

Which parts of this prayer feel especially poignant for
your life today?

Why is that?

Self knowledge

In my life I have found that the most secure, mature people are those who know themselves well and have deep and clear self-knowledge.

Some people travel through life constantly surprised by themselves. They operate such busy, plate-spinning lives that they don't stop to reflect or work out why they think or act a certain way. Then the plates fall down and give them, and those around them, a real headache! Many of us are like this. We can floored by the slightest thing. We feel uncertain, not just of life around us, but also of our own ability to cope with the challenges thrown at us.

One of the best ways we can get to know ourselves is to spend time reflecting, with the help of an accountability partner or mentor.

Over the years I know that I have really benefitted from the comments and questions my mentors have levelled at me.

I don't pretend these are easy things to find out. But I do believe them to be highly necessary.

For example, if you don't have someone who can say to you, "Why did you act that way? What impact did that behaviour have on others around you?" then perhaps you won't really ever deal with certain aspects of your character.

If you don't yet have a mentor and would like to know more about how you tick, I have written some self-reflection questions that you might find helpful in Appendix E.

What does the Bible say about self-knowledge? Well, it is clear that we should take time to look at how we are acting and thinking. It warns us to test ourselves in order to live wisely and impact others well.

1 Timothy 4:16 (ESV) says, *"Keep a close watch on yourself and on the teaching. Persist in this, for by so doing you will save both yourself and your hearers."*

I have also worked out that one of the things I need in order to be stable and understand myself more deeply, is regular time with other people who struggle in the same areas I do. Some people might call it a recovery group. Praying and talking with these precious people each week has made a massive difference to my life. I can honestly say that it has totally changed all of us.

One of our members has written what meeting up over the last year has meant for her. She says,

"Our group has been so influential for me. My friends here have spoken life and truth into me and make sure that my head and heart are in the right place. I have learned that being me is a wonderful thing. In fact, I am absolutely beautiful! Whereas I have spoken lies over myself all my life, they have spoken truth. That is priceless."

Proverbs 20:5 (ESV) says, *"The purpose in a man's heart is like deep water, but a man of understanding will draw it out."*

Are you surrounding yourself with people of understanding and wisdom? Are you providing that for others? Perhaps that is something you need to think about today.

Self-control

I believe that the most fought-over ground in the whole world is the few centimetres between our ears! Our minds are constantly warring with us and this is where the enemy will attack us most.

Many of us have a peculiarly undeveloped part of our brains. It is the part where discipline lives! We really struggle to keep on doing what we know to be right over any period of time. We start strong, but then veer off course when life gets hard or when something tricky comes to strike us.

The good news is that 2 Timothy 1:7 (NLT) says, *"For the Spirit God gave us does not make us timid, but gives us power, love and self-discipline."*

Other versions use the term "sound judgment". Wouldn't you like to have self-discipline and sound judgment when it comes to making decisions about how you live? Wouldn't you love not to live in fear and timidity about your old ways any more? Well you can!

Recently, my four children and I were doing a family quiet time about the story in 1 Kings 3 where Solomon is asked by two mothers to determine which one is a baby's true mother.

At the end I asked the kids what they felt God was saying to them through the passage. One of my three sons, Ben, thought for a while, then he told me that by asking for wisdom, Solomon had made the best choice. King, Solomon hadn't asked for power, riches, or favour in battle.

Ben said that by asking for wisdom he had asked God for an "empty box" and God was able to fill it with all the things he needed. I was really moved by that profound insight from a 9-year-old boy.

Maybe you have a box and it is full of all sorts of things. But, perhaps some of those things are not things you should be carrying right now?

Maybe you need to ask God for some wisdom today. Perhaps you need wisdom about your health, or your family or a friendship that has become painful. Maybe you need wisdom about your job or your past or your future. When we have wisdom and understanding we won't make bad choices. We won't fall into unhelpful and unhealthy habits.

1 Corinthians 6:12 says, *"All things are lawful for me," but not all things are helpful."*

Maybe you need some help to distinguish what you can and can't do. Potentially, God may need to show you the tree in your garden that separates you from Him.

Like our need for pleasure, the search for self-control all too often becomes distorted. Do you remember back in Genesis when God created the Garden of Eden and asked Adam and

Eve to look after it, to tend it?

In Genesis 1:25 (NABRE) we read

"God made every kind of wild animal, every kind of tame animal, and every kind of thing that crawls on the ground. God saw that it was good. Then God said: Let us make human beings in our image, after our likeness. Let them have dominion over the fish of the sea, the birds of the air, the tame animals, all the wild animals, and all the creatures that crawl on the earth. God created mankind in his image; in the image of God he created them; male and female he created them. God blessed them and God said to them: Be fertile and multiply; fill the earth and subdue it."

So at the beginning, God made things well and saw that "it was good". His creation gave Him pleasure. He then gave Adam and Eve the ability and permission to take enjoyment in the garden, but also some control over what He had made. But the garden was never totally theirs. It was shared. God still walked in it and spoke with them. He hadn't just left them to it. In a sense, their control was also made "in God's image".

We spend much of our lives trying to look for things we can control outside of God. We think that somehow "control" will guarantee us the life we are looking for; that feeling powerful will make us satisfied. But if we examine it closely, anxiety and fear are drivers for those who seek control. People who want to control everything are constantly striving, stressed and uptight. Like Martha in Luke 10, they are hard work to be around and many people will just want to get out of their way. Controlling people are often lonely and complain of being misunderstood. Not only that, but when they finally feel in control of a situation they have no need of God. He is effectively rendered unnecessary. When we try to control things outside of the way God operates, we will come unstuck.

How are you doing?

Are there areas of your life where you feel like you're battling for control?

How does that make you feel and why?

In what ways could seeking control be bad for your relationship with God?

Conversely, how could self-control help you this week?

Balance

Many of us struggle with balance. The phrase, "a little of what you fancy does you good" might be one we use, but most of us can't keep it to a "little". In fact, a "little" becomes a "lot" quite fast. Before you know it, the whole chocolate cake is gone, the whole film has been watched, the whole hour you set aside to pray or exercise has been swallowed up by something else. Some of us need a restraining order put in place over our hearts don't we?!

The Bible tells us that, *"Whoever fears God will avoid all extremes"* (Ecclesiastes 7:18 NIV). I can't tell you how happy I was when I found that verse! It was literally LIFE GIVING for me. You see, that one little scripture told me that I didn't have to be led by my feelings, or my hormones, or my circumstances, or my past. I didn't have to be swayed by my friendships or my struggles or my hang-ups. I didn't have to be extreme in my outlook, or my character. It told me that it was possible to be *balanced*.

So what does that mean? What does that phrase look

like in your life right now? What are the extremes in your behaviour, character and habit life?

For me, this is something I have had to face and face hard. I knew that I was extremely controlled by food. I knew that there was no balance and order in that area of my life.

I knew that I operated in extremes in terms of my social life. I either kept myself to myself or partied so hard I got ill.

All of us can be prone to extremes. It is one of the devil's favourite places for us to inhabit. Living in extremism is when we make large errors of judgement. It is when we are liable to listen to the wrong voices and make the wrong choices.

I want my life to be one characterised by balance. I don't want to be hard work for those around me. I don't want to be so up and down that I am emotionally exhausted and drained or life-sappingly selfish for others.

Many of us feel squashed and suffocated by our lives. We run round like scalded cats, never still enough to think well. At times like this our lives can feel like a mattress. A mattress is comfortable if you lie on it. But it is never comfortable if it lies on you.

How are you doing?

Do you feel that you are extreme in any area of your life right now?

In what areas are you feeling suffocated by your habits?

What do you wish with all your heart to have dominion over?

Jesus' life shows us much about balance. No matter how busy or tired He was, He got up early and went to pray. He knew where His strength came from.

Some of us are weakened by our lack of time with the Lord. We have complained of stress or overwork, but what we are really experiencing is a power supply failure. We all know that when we see the "low battery" sign flash up on our phone screen that we need to plug it in. Otherwise things will be lost.

If we don't plug ourselves in to God on a regular basis we will not function well as people. We will not be balanced or consistent. Something important in us will be lost too.

Staying power

We have talked about breaking habits and letting go of things that are bad for us in earlier chapters. We know that our habits have the ability to heal us or hurt us and that as Christians, we need to be people who emulate Jesus and who live in the freedom He offers us. So how do we do this?

There are habits that will bless our lives. If we are honest, most of us know what they are. But we avoid working hard at them, because they are such hard work! Then we wonder why we are unhappy and why frustration and dissatisfaction can gnaw at our souls.

Some of us are great at beginning things well. But deep down we also know that the life well-lived is one that chooses to finish strong too. It doesn't count if we have granola for breakfast, but then three large pizzas for lunch! As we have said, it is easy to slip back into bad habits that we thought we had dealt with, especially if we are in a cycle of dependency.

Philippians 3:13-15 (NIV) says,

"Brothers and sisters, I do not consider myself yet to have taken hold of it. But one thing I do: Forgetting what

is behind and straining toward what is ahead, I press on toward the goal to win the prize for which God has called me heavenward in Christ Jesus."

Each of us needs to keep pushing forward, straining towards the goal and pressing on, especially when we feel like giving up.

Recently, I was listening to a talk by Dr Caroline Leaf who is a wonderful Christian cognitive neuroscientist. As part of her sermon she read this passage from Romans 7:23 (MSG) which says,

"The moment I decide to do good, sin is there to trip me up. I truly delight in God's commands, but it's pretty obvious that not all of me joins in that delight. Parts of me covertly rebel, and just when I least expect it, they take charge. I've tried everything and nothing helps. I'm at the end of my rope. Is there no one who can do anything for me? Isn't that the real question? The answer, thank God, is that Jesus Christ can and does. He acted to set things right in this life of contradictions where I want to serve God with all my heart and mind, but am pulled by the influence of sin to do something totally different."

She was talking about the ways in which we can change our behaviours and, with God's help, rewire our brains. It is so comforting to know that God can and will help us in this. More than this, He will help us to help ourselves.

The thing that God wants most for us is to raise us up on the last day. He doesn't want us limping to the finish, battered and bruised by life's knocks and curveballs. He has plans to prosper us, not harm us, plans for our hope and our future (see Jeremiah 29:11).

You can choose to live your life so well that you finish

strong. You can decide that you will not be a quitter. That same verse I quoted earlier, Philippians 3:14 in a different version, the ESV says, *"I press on toward the goal for the prize of the upward call of God in Christ Jesus."*

You have an "upward" call on your life! It is to make the choices God is empowering you to make, for His sake and His glory. So decide today to press on and move up.

Keep going! You can do it!

Chapter 6
The Healed Life

"Nothing paralyzes our lives like the attitude that things can never change. We need to remind ourselves that God can change things. Outlook determines outcome. If we see only the problems, we will be defeated; but if we see the possibilities in the problems, we can have victory."
–Warren Wiersbe

As we have said in earlier chapters, it is possible for us to be set free from addiction. Romans 6:13-14 (ESV) tells us that as Christians, sin does not get the final say. It will not have dominion over us.

"Do not present the parts of your body to sin as instruments of wickedness, but present yourselves to God, as those who have been brought from death to life; and present the parts of your body to Him as instruments of righteousness. For sin shall not be your master, because you are not under law but under grace."

Much of what you will read in the coming pages is devoted to telling the stories of people who share how they have come under grace, coped with their problems and found healing through their relationships with God and His people.

These stories cover many addictions, such as approval, alcohol, drugs, self-harm, gambling, dysfunctional relationships, eating disorders and pornography. I am immensely grateful to all those who have been interviewed for this book – both those who chose to remain anonymous and those who have agreed for their name to be printed.

We begin our journey with Tracey, who bravely shares her story of complex addictions with us.

Freedom from dysfunction
Tracey's story

When did you know you had a problem with addictive behaviours?
Tracey: It took me a long time to know the truth about my addictions. I'd deal with one, believe I was free, but still behave in a dysfunctional way. I then quickly had new addictions. In recovery this is referred to as a "discontent abstainer" or a "dry drunk".

My life had become unmanageable. I lived in denial about how bad the issues were. Things got out of control. I knew I needed help but I couldn't stop by myself. I didn't know how to, or if there was even a cure.

How did the problems all start for you?
Tracey: Around age 14 I was drinking alcohol and sniffing substances to escape from stuff. From then on I had addictive behaviours, which I used to get through difficult times in my life. I had post-natal depression, clinical depression, and a string of dysfunctional domestic violence relationships. My bad habits formed around these issues.

Overwhelmed by my emotions, the addictions were a way of managing and escaping hurt, pain, rejection, emptiness and low self-esteem.

What impact did that have on you and others around you?
Tracey: My mood fluctuated so I had a lot of poor relationships with others. My family lost trust in me and I lost hope in myself. This was a vicious circle of hurting. They say that "hurt people hurt people". It's true! This created a big impact on my mental health, physical health and general wellbeing. I suffered with financial loss. I nearly lost my home. I'd been homeless previously. I was left with scars, mentally and physically.

How did you feel about your issues?
Tracey: I felt ashamed of myself, guilty and a failure. I struggled to come to terms with what I had become. A man told me I was "damaged goods". I felt broken and at times unrepairable.

Did you tell anyone about your problems, or did you try to hide them?
Tracey: Over the years I hid some behaviours but other problems were more outward and obvious. A long time ago in the past I was hospitalised.

More recently, over the last 19 years, I have managed to work full time in an intense role, but behind the scenes in cycles I have lived in abuse, dysfunction and addiction.

What steps did you take towards your own recovery?
Tracey: My first step to recovery was to admit to myself that I was struggling and couldn't stop it all by myself.

I had to put some plans and boundaries in place i.e. for my gambling I decided to hand over my bank card. I had to be accountable to someone. For my obsessive use of dating sites I had to block numbers and sites from my devices.

I sought help from trusted family members and church leaders. I found other distractions. I got into a group of like-minded people at church and prayed. I had to let go of control.

How long was that journey? What was helpful along the way?
Tracey: The journey has been going on for quite a while now. It's ongoing. For me, it's a daily recovery journey that I am on. I take one day at a time. All I have is today. I surrender and hand over to God, my higher power. I talk. I attend groups. I have a mentor. I keep a diary. I pray. I believe and I do it! I have changed who I spend time with too. Some things have changed suddenly and quickly and some things are taking longer.

I am free from gambling, and an obsession with a guy I was involved with. I am also free from living in a ten-year dysfunctional relationship and am also now free from self-harm! These different things have taken varied amounts of time, from almost a year, to 15 years.

The closer I walk with Jesus and accept I am free and I don't need those things to fulfill my life, the more they fall away from me. I have learnt that it is not in my own strength or power, or in my will to change. It is in His will. He strengthens me.

How would you describe yourself now Tracey? How do you think God sees you?
Tracey: I think I am someone who is being set free. I am a new creation and I am walking out of bad habits. I still have things to let go of, but I am set free from so much. I am forgiven!

I have new interests in life. I've tried new things. I fear less and because of that I can think of others more and serving encourages me.

I think God sees me as His child who has come home. He sees me as perfect in His sight. I was lost, but now I'm found.

This verse means a lot to me:

"'For I know the plans I have for you,' declares the Lord,

'plans to prosper you and not to harm you, plans to give you hope and a future.'" (Jeremiah 29-11)

What would you say to someone who describes themselves as an "addict" of any substance or addiction?
Tracey: I would say that the first thing is to recognise that you can't overcome this on your own. Acknowledge God's power and the power of the Holy Spirit
Then pray.
He can deliver you. Don't lose hope! It can take time. If you slip, get up again and ask God for forgiveness. Ask for help to cut off from distractions if needed, or from other people who may tempt you. We can't do it on our own, our chains need to be broken. It's not in our own strength but, *"We can do all things through Christ who strengthens us"* (Philippians 4:13).

Anxiety happens because we feel we have to figure it all out ourselves. The good news is we don't have to do that! God has a plan for us when we turn it all over to Him. Our job is to trust.

Talk to people who are like-minded and who have overcome. Be accountable to someone you trust. Remember that you are not defined by your habits and mistakes or your past. Trust and believe.

Are there any songs or verses of Scripture that have been key in your recovery?
Tracey: Yes. These songs have really blessed me:
1. "I'm no longer a slave to fear, I am a child of God" (Bethel)
2. You make me brave (Bethel)
3. Amazing Grace (John Newton)
4. Oceans (Hillsong United)
Verses that have helped me are:
"I am a new creature in Christ." (2 Corinthians 5:17)

"I am the temple of the Holy Spirit; I am not my own." (1
  Corinthians 6:19)

And this story from John 5:5-9:

*"One who was there had been an invalid for thirty-eight
years. When Jesus saw him lying there and learned that he
had been in this condition for a long time, he asked him, 'Do
you want to get well?'*

*'Sir,' the invalid replied, 'I have no one to help me into the
pool when the water is stirred. While I am trying to get in,
someone else goes down ahead of me.'*

*Then Jesus said to him, 'Get up! Pick up your mat and
walk.' At once the man was cured; he picked up his mat and
walked."*

*[Tracey Sweetman is a single parent of one daughter, aged
25. She works in mental health supporting people through
recovery to connect in the community, to achieve their
aspirations, through courses, employment, groups and faith.
She is involved in serving at her own church and attends a
church-based recovery group]*

How are you doing?

Which parts of what Tracey said strike a chord with
you?

Why do you think that is?

Do you feel as though you have experienced anything
similar?

What encourages you about her journey?

What do you feel you could access from her advice to help yourself at this time?

I feel a deep sense of privilege that Tracey felt able to speak out here about her issues. I just know that her story is going to bless people who read it.

Freedom from approval addiction
Josh's story

Tell me when you realised you had a problem with addictive behaviours.
Josh: I guess I never realised I had a problem until I became a Christian when I was 18 years old. You don't realise you are sleeping until you wake up! I started to realise the spiritual consequences of what I was doing and how it had created patterns of behaviour in me that thrived on an "addictive personality". I think that ultimately this addictive personality stemmed from struggling to be accepted by others.

How did that start for you?
Josh: I remember being quite popular with friends and particularly girls in primary school from the age of around 7 years old until I hit high school aged 11. From my first day in high school I was badly bullied and singled-out. Girls didn't find me attractive and I struggled being in a Grammar school that focused on being clever and academic, when I was more creative and outgoing. This created a really strong desire inside me to be accepted and loved.

What impact did that have on you?
Josh: It made me become someone I wasn't. I was having an identity crisis, probably like most teenagers do. However, mine seemed worse than everyone else's because they had friends to work it out with. It made me angry and violent towards others, ultimately leading me to take drugs, drink heavily and start exploring sex at the age of 14.

How did you feel about your problems?
Josh: I think if you'd asked me then, I would have told you I didn't have any issues or that I couldn't help my behaviour! I would never accept responsibility for my actions, so I never really saw what I was doing as an issue or a problem. I was just doing whatever felt right to me and gave me some sort of temporary high or good feeling.

Did you let anyone know about what you were going through, or did you try to keep it all hidden?
Josh: My parents were both pastors of a church, so I tried to hide everything, although I wasn't very good at it. They knew I was being bullied, but never knew how serious it was.

What steps did you take towards your own recovery?
Josh: Being honest, I didn't want to recover Ems! I wanted to be worse. I wanted to take more drugs, get drunk all the time and sleep with as many girls as possible. I was addicted to this lifestyle. But Jesus stepped into my world. I didn't want God, but He wanted me. That's what changed everything for me. I started to realise it wasn't the individual things I was doing that I was addicted to (smoking, drugs, drinking, sex etc), it was ultimately this desire to be accepted. So I had to dig into the Bible, go to as many church services and worship sessions as possible to connect to Jesus, because I knew He held the keys to my freedom.

How long was that journey for you? What helped?

Josh: It was about 4 years until I came to a place where I realised that who I am is OK. More than this, that I am accepted by God. I am a child of the Creator of the Universe. My life has significance. I have a purpose and I am here for a reason. The Bible was amazingly helpful, there are so many scriptures that point to us being loved (John 3:16, Romans 8:38-39, Galatians 3:26) and accepted (John 6:37, Colossians 3:12, Galatians 5:1). Being part of a church and a Christian community was immensely helpful, to be around similar, like-minded people who are all being healed by Jesus from a broken past. The worst thing you can do is be alone.

How would you describe yourself now Josh? How do you think God sees you?

Josh: I know that I don't have to let my past determine, define, or destroy my future anymore. I am aware of my past, so I don't put myself in unhelpful situations because none of us are perfect or above temptation. However, the power of Jesus has broken every chain that held me back in life, so I won't let my past haunt me. I am not an addict! I am free, I am whole, and it all stems from being loved by Jesus. Sometimes I struggle with how God sees me because of my past and my everyday mistakes, but I have faith to believe what the Bible says God sees in me. God sees greatness in me! He sees a world changer, a fighter, a lover, a committed husband, a devoted father and a passionate follower of Jesus. I see it now too because He gave me eyes to see.

What would you say to someone who told you they were an "addict"?

Josh: I would say the only thing I have any confidence in. There is a way out and His name is Jesus! It might be clichéd or unpopular, but I can't hide or lie about who changed me.

I couldn't help myself or change myself and, in all honesty and love, you can't change yourself either. Only Jesus can truly transform a life and take you from being broken to whole, bound to free, dead to alive.

Are there any key songs or verses of Scripture that have helped you?

Josh: There were two things that were extremely significant for me. Firstly, there is a song that fully broke through everything for me. It's called *Deliverer* by Bryn Waddell. In the middle of the song, God led him to say these words which really spoke to me: "There's someone here who has been bound to the same issues for years, but I'm telling you tonight that the power of Jesus is in this building!" Then he sang, "Your blood is enough to break every chain." Honestly, since I heard that whilst I was driving my car, 5 years ago, I have been completely free. Not perfect but free. Then secondly, this phrase, "Don't let your past determine your future." The Holy Spirit spoke these words to me when I woke from a dream where I was scared about my past coming back to ruin everything for me. Those words gave me peace and all the fear of going back to my past life left me forever.

[Josh Green is part of Manchester-based band Twelve24. He travels all over the world, performing music and inspiring thousands of young people with his story and the good news of Jesus. Josh is husband to Emma and has two young children, Liberty and Simeon]

How are you doing?

As you read Josh's story was there anything you could relate to?

What was it?

How do you feel about Josh's understanding that he was "free but not perfect?"

Is that your experience?

Do you want it to be? Why?

What aspects of Josh's advice do you think you might benefit from?

What could you do about that?

Freedom from Pornography
Bethany's story

When did you know you had a problem with addiction?
Bethany: When I got to university I suddenly had lots of free time and my own unrestricted space, money and technology. After realising that pornography probably wasn't the best way to spend my time, I decided to stop watching it, but found that I couldn't and I knew then that the roots of this issue were deep.

How did it start for you?
Bethany: At the age of 9 I had a school sex education lesson and when I was home, I Googled "masturbation" and saw

images and videos that shocked me. As a teenager, I was confused about sex and my sexuality and, receiving no other input on the matter, I turned to porn to educate and then to self-soothe my feelings of loneliness, confusion and shame.

What impact did that have on you and others around you?
Bethany: The more porn I watched, the more lies I told to cover my tracks, which meant that it was difficult to build really strong, honest relationships with family and friends. I avoided romantic relationships and, after experiencing the danger of attempting to satisfy myself with flings, turned back to porn as the "safe" option.

How did you feel about your issue?
Bethany: On the surface, I was a well-educated, confident "good Christian girl", but inside I felt intense amounts of shame, guilt and fear. I was so ashamed that porn was even an issue for me as a woman and felt so guilty that I had told lies and done things that I didn't want to. But, most of all, I was afraid that other people would find out and reject me. This fear of rejection kept me in the addiction cycle for over a decade.

Did you tell anyone about your problem?
Bethany: For over 10 years I managed to keep parents, friends, housemates, church leaders and mentors totally in the dark about my struggle. The secrecy of the addiction made it even more appealing in times of temptation. When I eventually told someone, there was such relief and the burden became lighter.

What steps did you take towards your own recovery?
Bethany: When I first recognised that I had a problem, I set myself goals and downloaded software on to my computer,

but I would constantly fall at the first hurdle. The first real step in my journey of recovery was telling my small group leader who was able to share her own experiences, offer encouragement and keep me accountable.

How long was that journey? What was helpful along the way?
Bethany: From the point of sharing with my small group leader until the moment I could say, "Wow! I am free!" was about two years. The turning point for me was the prayer ministry sessions I received from my pastor's wife which allowed me to delve deep and untangle the roots of the addiction. After those four intense, heart-wrenching and emotional sessions, I felt as though I had been freed.

How would you describe yourself now? How do you think God sees you?
Bethany: God has completely transformed my brokenness and now uses me to speak light and hope as I work for a charity dedicated to dealing with the issue of porn! He has healed my wounds and filled my emptiness and has taught me what it is to be His child. He has taught me, so patiently, what it is to be loved and to love someone else.

What would you say to someone who described themselves as an "addict" of any substance or problem like pornography?
Bethany: It's so important to remember that your identity is not bound up in having an addiction. Watching porn or taking drugs may be something that you *do*, but it is not who you *are*. In order to move forward and into recovery, it's essential to place your identity in Christ rather than in the problem.

Are there any songs or verses of Scripture that have been key in your recovery?
Bethany: Songs that have helped me are:

Healer (Hillsong)
Desert Song (Hillsong)
We Will Run (Gungor)
When Peace Like a River (Philip Paul Bliss)
You Are My Strength (Hillsong United)
Bible verses that have blessed me are:
Romans 8
Zechariah 4:6
Psalm 27

[Bethany MacDonald is the Schools and Youth Development worker for Visible Ministries. Bethany's role is to work full time for the "Naked Truth" project developing and delivering lessons and materials on pornography in schools and providing tools and training for youth leaders.]

How are you doing?

Does anything in Bethany's story ring true in your own life?

In what ways do you think you are like her?

What gives you hope as you read her story?

What parts of her recovery do you think you would do well to mimic?

What could you do next about this?

Chapter 7
My Story of Dirty Eating

"Give us this day our daily bread."
(Matthew 6:11)

I always had a bizarre relationship with food. I loved it and I hated it. I sometimes struggled to eat things that were good for me. I had huge weaknesses when it came to eating. Maybe you do too?

Food for me had always been far too important. It was the thing that defined my day. My three meals were often planned before I even got out of bed. It was definitely an idol – something I was preoccupied with and gave far too much importance.

I was put on my first diet at two years old. My mum said she didn't know what to do with me when I cried, so she fed me. I'm not blaming her for my problems, because she did her best with me. I think my issues about food were just very complicated.

Every prayer book I kept was filled with prayers where I begged God for help with my eating. There were years when I overate and put on huge amounts. And a few leaner years when I was often at the doctors and was weighed every week because I was not eating enough and was making myself sick regularly. My body suffered in the way most bodies do when they go through erratic eating problems. I didn't have regular periods. I was constantly cold and had poor circulation. I had aches and pains.

I tried every single food fad – even a tangerine diet where I ate so many tangerines that my skin (especially my knees, knuckles and cheeks) went bright orange. I looked as though I had undergone an unfortunate spray-tan administered by someone wearing a blindfold!

I read diet books. I tried many odd food combinations. But I could never stick to anything. As an adult, and even until very recently, I was obsessed with my scales and weighed myself most days. Sometimes more than once.

A couple of years ago I had a health scare when I found a lump on my breast. My doctor said I was fine, but suggested weight loss would reduce my risk of cancer. That was it. That impacted me and scared me. Then the same week I was walking home from dropping the children off at school when I saw a sign outside a local clinic. It said,

"Hypnotherapy gastric band therapy sessions available here."

I was taken aback, "HYPNO WHAT?!"

I thought about that for a minute and felt angry. I don't believe in hypnotherapy. I believe in the power of God! I wondered if maybe I could ask the Holy Spirit to help me to know when I was full (something I had never known) and to be my "gastric band"? So I did just that. I felt almost instant change. I started to feel uncomfortable if ever I overate. I started to eat less and feel more full. I couldn't believe that I had reached the age of 41 without anyone ever telling me I could ask this of the Holy Spirit!

I made a deal with God that day: if He could find me a personal trainer who was a normal human being and not some kind of super-athlete, then I would try to lose weight permanently. (But then I added on to the deal that this person had to be female, a Christian, and someone who would not charge any money!) That all seemed vastly unlikely. I felt I was pretty safe!

But God was giggling. The following week I went to a women's event at church. A girl called Claire stood up at the end and said she was a Personal Trainer. I slid down into my seat and my heart raced. Someone in Heaven was smiling. But I was having a mild panic attack.

I took the incredibly bold step of going very near Claire that night. I stood behind her for around two whole seconds. Then I found myself walking away very fast and then running to my car.

I felt ashamed of my problems. I wanted to be free of them. But asking someone to help me in such a personal and involved way seemed too hard and awkward. What if she said no? What if she said yes?

The next week at church there she was again, all smiley and fit and ready. I walked up to her and shyly asked if she would help me. I felt like I was asking someone on a date with me somewhere I didn't want to go.

Before she agreed to meet with me, Claire sent me a detailed set of questions to fill in so she could assess my needs. The questionnaire she gave me asked me all sorts of things such as:

Did I eat when I was unhappy? The answer was yes.
Did I eat when I was angry? Yes.
Did I eat to reward myself for doing well at something? Yes.
Did I eat when I had accidentally hurt someone? Yes.
Did I eat when I was full? Yes.
Did I eat when I was hungry? Yes.

I realised FOR THE FIRST TIME IN MY LIFE that eating was my comfort, my punishment, my delight, my enemy, my friend and my answer to almost all my problems in my life. The problem was, it was an answer that wasn't working.

I need to go a bit further back here and give you a little bit of my history. In 2001 following some serious back pain, I had gone for a series of scans which showed that I had been born with facet joint spondylosis in my vertebrae and sacrilisation. That's posh medical talk that means that one of the bones in my back is fused to the triangular bone at the base of my spine. The doctors also discovered that on the left side I have a bone fracture which has come away from the main spine. Any exercise I did seemed to make this condition worse. I'd had poor mobility, spasms in my legs, and intermittent back pain for years.

Claire met with me every Friday for the next six months. I had never exercised until that point because of my bad back, so this poor girl had her work cut out! Claire had to take away my fear of pain as well as all the stiffness in my joints. I soon found that the more movement I endured, the less pain I had. For the next few months I had some totally pain free days for the first time in a number of years.

This was the start of my journey towards my freedom. And I will always be so grateful to Claire for starting me off on this new lease of life. Claire enabled me to lose a stone and a half and get fitter. I joined a gym and signed up for some classes. I wobbled my way through aqua-aerobics, step classes and even took up jogging. For the first time in my life, when I looked in the mirror I felt a sense of pride. I was eating less, moving more and was almost pain free.

But then, when I wasn't able to see Claire anymore, old habits tried to come back hard and I had to fight them. Fortunately I had new tools in my armoury.

Start Monday

The comedian, Peter Kay, talks about the "Start Monday" diet.

The trouble is, there are 52 Mondays per year! Stuffing your face with chocolate on Friday is not going to make you feel great on Monday. Getting totally plastered at the weekend won't make for a good start to the week.

In Romans 12:1 the Bible talks about us being a "living sacrifice". What does that mean? I think it means we have to sacrifice things whilst we are alive. We have to make adjustments in order to live well, or there will be consequences.

Did you know that in 2013 it was estimated that more than 1.6 million people in the UK were affected by eating disorders? There are apparently more deaths from eating disorders than from any other mental illness, and it is estimated that 10% of all sufferers die as a result of their condition. I didn't want to be a statistic like that. I don't want that for you either.

I know that I can't operate a "Start Monday" kind of existence. I can't put off what I want out of life. I have to start today. I needed to learn to sacrifice what I wanted to put into my mouth now in order to ensure I would be around to care for my husband and my kids.

Is clean eating really dirty?

I just want to share some of the things I have learnt (the hard way) about the various diets on the market. As I have said, I have tried pretty much all of them and yo-yo-ed my way up the down the numbers on the scales for years.

I have noticed a huge rise, as I am sure you have too, in the "clean eating" phenomenon. Clean eating as a THING has exploded and become an enormous industry within the food world. I am all for healthy eating, but many of these books and blogs look a bit too much like eating disorders in disguise. They put a very pretty face on quite an ugly issue. They glorify denying yourself food groups that humans have been eating for 1000s of years.

From superfood Buddha bowls to courgette, wheatgrass

and bee pollen smoothies, never before have we been so concerned with the purity and provenance of our food. Ironically, it has become an unhealthy obsession.

Maybe we have bought the latest nutrition-based diet book by an amazing looking young woman who lives somewhere beautiful and has an immaculate kitchen and wonderfully stylish clothes. She shares with us her grain-free, sugar-free, dairy-free lifestyle, but the small print says, "I am not a dietician."

Did you know that anyone can be a nutritionist? It takes £29 and a short Internet course to become one. There is no vetting procedure. You could be one even if you had an eating disorder or a food addiction. You could pay your £29, set yourself up with a pretty little vlog and tell people to eat quails eggs and beetroot emulsion. No one would stop you.

And I am sorry to say that I have bought into this. I have been tempted by these clean eating fads of eating raw food, paleo food, gluten-free food, starch diets, carb-free diets and I even faithfully did a Whole30 programme (twice) as part of my research for this book. All of them promise miracles. And they do work, for a while. But I have learnt that it is not *sustainable* to eat in this way. Many of these diets are scientifically flawed and have potentially dangerous consequences. I have come to realise that praising myself for depriving myself of food groups that my body needs in the long term, is not healthy.

Othorexia is a recognised issue for many people. It is the obsession with eating foods that one considers healthy.

So please, can I ask you to take care?

If you are going to go on a diet, make sure it is one that lets you eat all the things that your body needs to thrive and grow and regenerate.

Romans 12: 1-2 in The Message says:

"So here's what I want you to do, God helping you: Take

your everyday, ordinary life—your sleeping, eating, going-to-work, and walking-around life—and place it before God as an offering. Embracing what God does for you is the best thing you can do for him. Don't become so well adjusted to your culture that you fit into it without even thinking. Instead, fix your attention on God. You'll be changed from the inside out. Readily recognize what he wants from you, and quickly respond to it. Unlike the culture around you, always dragging you down to its level of immaturity, God brings the best out of you, develops well-formed maturity in you."

Isn't that was you want? To be changed from the inside out? To be mature and not to relapse? I do. Because that is lasting change.

Let me tell you about some of the changes I have made over the last 2-3 years. I have had to make room for good habits in my shopping list and on my calendar, way before the food ends up in my cupboards and my drawers. Good habits take up space. They have to be incredibly intentional. You have to *step* into them. You don't suddenly find yourself out for a morning run, do you? You have to plan it. You have to buy trainers that fit you and lycra that holds you in or up. Then you have to lay your gym things out, so that you don't change your mind as easily the next day. You have to plan time in your diary and work schedule to exercise.

I have had to start to see myself differently. I have had to believe I will lose weight and not put it on again.

I have had to change my shopping list dramatically, say no to hanging out with certain friends who are a bad influence on my eating, worship God in the gym, refuse to buy or eat as much processed food, not keep certain foods in the house, not bake as much, cut down on cheese, and not eat sugar.

But it's all been so worth it, because I am healthier than

ever. I feel younger because I have more energy. I sleep better. My clothes fit me and I have more balance in my life. The best thing of all is that I have had whole months without any back pain. For me this has been life-changing!

I could not have kept on track without the help of the girls I meet with each week. We have laughed and cried a lot this past year as we have delved deeper into the mindsets that have held us back for years.

One of the girls who has met up with me each week has this to say about our group:

"For over 30 years I feel I have lived in the shadow of things other people have spoken over me. These were lies that, day-by-day, built up to become the truth of what I saw when I looked in the mirror. It's amazing how much those words played out in my mind. I went through life with a smile on my face, being the first to crack the joke and make people laugh, even if it was at my own expense. I was quite good at being the 'funny one', always enjoying the moment and having fun, but in the background those words were there in my mind. There were times when they have held me back, made me feel unlovable and unworthy.

Our group has been a safe place of loving friendship for me. We have shared our stories, our struggles, our successes and we have broken down those walls in our minds that have been built up over the years, through prayer and by speaking God's word over ourselves and encouraging each other. It's been a place where I have been loved for being me, but challenged to be more than I think I can be! It's been a place where I have begun to speak a new truth: that I am beautiful, that I am loved and that I am worthy. And it's a place where I have faced my fears with a greater confidence than before and the chains that bound me for so long have begun to drop off. I'm set free and I'm learning to live in the *freedom* that Jesus has given me!"

Something to declare

If I asked you what burdens you, I am sure you could all tell me. Maybe, like me, it's your weight, or maybe it's your anxiety, fear, depression, OCD, another addiction you can't kick, or a relationship you know is not good for you.

Just for a moment, imagine being at an airport, checking in your cases. The woman says, "Did you pack your bags yourself?" You look down at your burden and say, "I had some help. There was this thing that happened, or that person who said that..."

You are carrying all that around with you and it's heavy isn't it? Carrying heavy things affects the way we walk, our mood, our sleeping, our happiness, our eating – in fact, just about everything.

The woman says, "I'm sorry, but if you want to get on that plane you either have to pay for your excess baggage or you need to leave it behind."

Some of you are carrying *excess baggage* and all your life you have just been paying for it. You have said, "I can't leave this behind. This is who I am. I have always had an eating problem or this depression or this addiction. And I always will..." Then you pick it up and walk with it on your back, weighing down your heart.

But that is not right.

You can let it go.

You don't need that in your life any more.

I know I am still on my journey, but many of my old habits have gone and my thought processes have changed. A couple of years ago I couldn't run a bath without getting out of breath! But I can now run longer distances. It is easy for me to bosh out a 5 or 6k run in the morning. My kids can't remember what it was like to have a really unfit mum.

God's change for us is personal. He won't change me

like He wants to change you and vice versa. Each of us is different. Your struggle might not be with food, or your back. It might be with your addictions, your friendships, or your finances. You might have behaviours you wish to get rid of like nail biting, picking your spots or constantly comparing yourself to others. You might have irrational fears, suffer with panic attacks or night terrors. You might be addicted to diet drinks, or caffeine or going to the gym. But God can help you. He is the habit breaker! God's change is lasting and freeing. That doesn't mean we won't find it hard to give up what we have relied on, but it means we can have a new mindset and heavenly help with our issues.

So how can we help ourselves? How can we put down that excess baggage and walk into the future God has for us?

Ways to help ourselves:

1. Be careful who your friends are

There are certain people in your world who make temptation all that more appealing. You giving in to that cake or that drug or that drink makes their problem feel less, so they encourage you more. They will, in fact, be feeding your weaknesses. We need to be very discerning about who we share life with. Your weaknesses will be drawn to any friendship that accepts them and feeds them.

Temptation will bond you with the wrong people and make you uncomfortable in the presence of the right ones. This will ultimately sabotage God's plan for you. Many people have to make a break from those friendships and start again with helpful and encouraging people.

Have a think now about who is in your life that makes your habits worse. What could you do about that?

2. Be accountable

The moment I asked some friends who also struggle with

food to meet with me every week, to help us all overcome our eating disorders, was the moment God broke a chain of pride in me. Having to share with others where I stumbled and fell was so helpful. I meet with these girls almost every week. We keep in very regular contact and text each other to encourage one another or to ask for help and prayer. I believe this keeps me (and them) on track and helps me know people are checking up on my behaviour and attitudes.

3. Don't give up when you slip up
We are sometimes going to have days where we fail and fall back into old ways. If and when this happens, don't give up on your dreams of being free. Keep going. Pick yourself up and start again. Celebrate the ways in which you have changed and how far you have come. Don't berate yourself or condemn yourself for not being perfect. Don't think "I will start again tomorrow." Think, "I can start again right now."

4. Fast food
In Chapter 1, I spoke about the fact that we live in an easy access, instant-grabbing culture. One thing we can do to counteract that is to fast and pray. Using fasting we can teach ourselves to say no to something that is normally within reach for us. You don't have to fast from food. It could be that you give up coffee, or TV, or some other habit for a while.

Denying ourselves something starts to teach us that we will survive in spite of our cravings. We will learn that our temptations will pass. We start to realise that our bodies and our minds can manage without, and that we don't have to tune into every appetite we long for. We think we are weak, but actually this is not correct. The Bible tells us that, *"He that is in us is greater than he that is in the world"* (1 John 4:4). We don't need to be bossed around by our addictions any more.

5. Think long term

Sometimes you have to forget what you want *now* and remember what you deserve or hope for later. Denying yourself short term pleasure to gain long term pride is a great strategy for change. Keep a list of all the things you will gain when you are free, or do the exercise below. Remind yourself of this often. Keep a record of your tiny victories. For example, each time you choose not to drink or smoke. Or if you decide to have a salad and not a cream cake, make a note of it. Next time you are tempted, you will see a growing self-history of discipline and self-control.

6. Encourage yourself

Leave notes around your home motivating you. Perhaps put your goals somewhere you can tick them off, or make notes when you experience changes. Think about your victories and focus on how far you have come. Give yourself treats that are NOT related to your addiction. For example, don't celebrate losing a stone by going to grab a burger! Get yourself a new purse or a prayer journal or that new book you've wanted to read.

How are you doing?

This is an exercise that can help you think about the long-term benefits of stopping your addiction.

Focus on the enormous sense of wellbeing you would feel if you were free of your addiction. Write down any benefits you would experience. Think about your positive changes in terms of your bank balance, your health, your relationships, your happiness and your mood.

What would that feel like for you?

Think about how much more energy you would have throughout the day and how much better you would sleep at night.

What impact would less anxiety have in your life?

What would it feel like to have a sharper memory?

What would it be like to have more times of relaxation without any negative side effects?

What long-term effects would being free have on your self -image?

What impact would this have on your family? Your work? Your leisure time?

10 life hacks for addicts

Part of understanding ourselves means we need to be prepared for addictive pangs to strike and be ready to take swift action. Here are some 10-second addiction hacks I have found useful for when I feel I need distracting:

1. Pray. Even if your prayer is as short as the one word scream "HELP", or the three word "Take it away!" God hears and answers our prayers. Don't leave prayer as a last resort. Tell your Father what you need and how you feel.

2. Stress ball. Get yourself some beads or a rubber stress ball. Moving the beads or squeezing the ball back and forth between your fingers helps keeps your hands busy and removes tension.

3. Chew gum or suck a sweet. Keeping the mouth busy can help us not do something else like stress eat or smoke.

4. Write your thoughts down. Voicing your thinking either out loud or on paper can reduce the anxiety or overwhelming feelings that trigger many addictions. Declaring Scripture over ourselves is also a very useful and powerful tool against the lies we can sometimes find ourselves saying. The Bible teaches us to take *"every thought captive"* (2 Corinthians 10:5). This means we need to recognise our thoughts and realise if they are contrary to God's word to us. Once we do that, we need to OUT them! We need to "arrest" them, kick them out, and show them that Jesus is boss.

5. Self massage. Give yourself a quick massage – a brief hand massage or rolling a ball under your feet can massively reduce tension and help us to relax.

6. Smell something beautiful – keeping some perfume, a candle, or some essential oil near you can have a powerful effect on your emotions. Tests have shown that comforting smells can reduce anxiety and even lower our pulse rate. This can mean we are less stressed and therefore less liable to listen to or act on our cravings.

7. Exercise. Go for a walk or a run – exercise is a great distraction when we are tempted and helps take our mind off poor behaviours.

8. Steam. Use a sauna or steam room to help relieve tension and get rid of toxins in the body.

9. Apps. Download a recovery-related app on your smartphone. There are new ones coming onto the market all the time. "Recovery Box" is an amazing one that allows you to record your choices and show others what you have been up to. It helps you assess your triggers and score them too.

10. Make a gratitude list. Write down every single thing you are grateful for and re-read it every day – especially at times when you are tempted. Reminding yourself that you have a lot to be thankful for helps you think in a more balanced and consistent way.

Your story

Now that you have read my story and the stories of others in addictive cycles, and learnt some ways to help yourself, maybe you can begin to write your own recovery journey. Recording how you feel now can really help you begin to heal. It will also allow you to look back and see how much God has transformed you in the months ahead. Even on days when it is hard, you can remember that failure is a detour not a dead end. You can also share your story with me on my website. If you would like to, go to www.emshancock.com.

I hope that having read this chapter you feel more confident than ever that God will take on whatever problems you are facing and journey through them with you. Your freedom and healing is possible. More than that, it is on its way!

The next section looks at the behavioural addiction of OCD and offers strategies to help people who struggle on their onward march away from their compulsions.

Chapter 8
Freedom From OCD

"The best time to plant a tree was 20 years ago.
The second best time is now."
–Chinese proverb

I now want to talk about something that affects a large number of people, and that is OCD. Obsessive Compulsive Disorder is something that is slowly becoming more understood, but many people are still mystified by it. What do we mean by an obsession disorder like this?

We could call a compulsive obsession something that is a persistent impulse, image or thought that appears to hi-jack the mind and cause severe unease. Often people with OCD describe their anxiety as being based on thoughts that are uncomfortable, inappropriate, intrusive and even irrational. But knowing these things does not always give those people keys to help manage, resolve or allay those fears.

I know that whole books have been devoted to this problem and that it is a massively broad issue, encompassing many different behaviours that are personal to each individual. Therefore I am sorry if I don't do justice to the issues you are currently facing. My aim is that you will find some comfort and some challenge in this section that will help you consider the next step for you.

Some common issues sufferers struggle with include:

- Morbid apprehension
- Irrational thought patterns
- Fear of germs, catching or spreading infection
- Fear of poisons, bodily harm from materials, buildings, others.
- Nagging doubts connected with safety (Did I turn off the iron before I left the house? Did I shut the garage? Did I lock the door? Is the oven still on?)
- Hoarding and keeping hold of things that are no longer really needed
- The need to do certain tasks in a special order
- The need to unplug all appliances or check light switches
- Fear of disaster, trauma or accident
- Superstitious practices
- Repeated washing and other cleaning rituals
- Sexual or violent imagery or words coming into the mind without obvious provocation

Of course, just because we have thought one or more of these things at any time, does not mean we have OCD. Most of us will have had these kinds of impulses from time to time. And this is normal for us. There will be times of heightened anxiety for each of us that we can explain. But for OCD sufferers, these thoughts are not fleeting, nor can they be easily explained away. They are repeated, strong compulsions. They don't appear to give the person any choice. They "arrive" in the brain as fully-formed fears and cause immediate nervousness. They demand certain compulsions to be acted out, in order to soothe and calm the mind.

If you suffer with an obsession, you probably use some kind of mental process to try to compose yourself and reduce your worry levels. Maybe you count to 10, or write things down, or repeat calming behaviours until you feel pacified. If you are concerned about contamination and germs, you may resort to hand washing a large number of times a day in a fixed routine in order to reassure yourself. You have worked out that this is the best way to manage your problem. As it doesn't "harm" anyone else, you just stick with it. It works for you. Your compulsive behaviour eventually subsides.

But it can leave you confused and ashamed. You can feel alone and unable to share with others the odd things you have thought and experienced.

If you, or someone you know, are living with an obsession, I hope this next section of the book helps you to re-imagine what life could be like for you, or for them. I pray it helps you ask some deep questions of yourself and starts to help you formulate some answers. I also hope it provides you with biblical and practical tools for your healing.

I don't know if you have ever considered what the Bible says about OCD? Until I starting researching for this book, I confess that I had not even thought about whether it said anything at all. I was relieved and blessed to find that Scripture is so wonderfully helpful to us as we consider this particular addiction.

One of the most pertinent passages the Lord gave me that I feel speaks to the heart of those suffering with any kind of OCD is this one from Philippians 4:4-8 (ESV). It says:

"Rejoice in the Lord always; again I will say, Rejoice. Let your reasonableness be known to everyone. The Lord is at hand; do not be anxious about anything, but in everything by prayer and supplication with thanksgiving let your requests be made known to God. And the peace of God, which surpasses all understanding, will guard your hearts and your minds in Christ Jesus. Finally, brothers, whatever is true, whatever is honorable, whatever is just, whatever is

pure, whatever is lovely, whatever is commendable, if there is any excellence, if there is anything worthy of praise, think about these things."

Let's look at this passage bit by bit and sees what foundations it offers us:

1. The passage starts with rejoicing, followed by more rejoicing. *"Rejoice in the Lord always; again I will say, Rejoice."* For the OCD sufferer the opposite is the case. The person will start with an obsession or fear and then repeat that fear over and over in their minds. Notice the verse says, "I WILL say." Our wills are very active when we suffer from addiction. We can feel as though we are fighting with ourselves. This verse shows us how important the mind is in the battle against addictive thinking. What we allow ourselves to think about and dwell on is so vital. If we have rejoicing in our minds, we won't have room for all those fears to get in. You might say, "But Ems, how can I rejoice when I'm panicking or obsessing?" I think the answer is to keep trusting in the Jesus who said to the woman in Mark 5:34, *"Daughter, your faith has healed you. Go in peace and be freed from your suffering."* Think of this kind of thinking as like a soldier training for war in peacetime. It is putting something in your mind BEFORE worry can get in. It is anticipating what might come and not allowing it. This will give you a firm foundation for control of your mind.

2. The phrase "let your reasonableness be known to everyone" really jumped out at me. For most people with OCD, their lack of "reasonableness" – the fact that their behaviour appears not to make sense, even to them or to others who love them – is something that baffles them. One of my friends told me that she had to say a number in a certain way each time she saw it. If she didn't, she would

feel anxious. She knew this was silly and irrational, but she couldn't seem to help it. A young boy I spoke to recently, told me he had to tap his bed a number of times before he could feel calm enough to fall asleep.

Another lady spoke of accidentally banging her arm really hard. As an OCD sufferer, she had such an obsession with symmetry that she felt she needed to bang the other one to "make it fair". So she repeated the behaviour, even though she knew it would hurt her even more. Now for many of us, this kind of action appears nonsensical. Why would anyone deliberately hurt themselves in this way? Why would we be so set on doing something we know does not make sense?

It is because deep down, the person has a buried fear of what might happen if they do not "obey" the compulsion within them. Often these fears go back to childhood. They have a grain of truth about them, but may have been drastically blown out of proportion.

If you suffer with OCD, perhaps a prayer you could pray is that you will begin, like this verse says, to be "reasonable" in your thinking, and that you will one day actually be known for this. You could also pray that God begins to reveal any hidden or buried worry that triggers your behaviours.

3. Next we come to a wonderfully comforting phrase, "The Lord is at hand." This simply means God is near us. He will never allow us to be alone. As we have said a number of times, addictions of all kinds often start in places of isolation or loneliness. If we can remember that God is near us, with us, IN us even, we can relax. If He is present we don't need to fear. If He is present we are understood, loved and known. If He is present then we are protected. Maybe we need to tell ourselves over and over again, "God is here. God is near. I am not alone right now. He knows me. He loves me. He sees me." Because this is the truth.

4. Then comes a specific instruction, a command even. "Do not be anxious about anything." There is no wiggle room here. There is no asterisk added, no small print that allows for your type of anxiety to sneak its way in! There are no exceptions to this rule. As the people of God, we are not meant to be anxious – full stop. If we find ourselves habouring anxiety, dwelling on anxious thoughts, or repeating anxious patterns in our minds, we can remind ourselves of the powerful truth of this verse.

5. Next there is something we can do about our fears. The verse encourages us, saying, "but in everything by prayer and supplication with thanksgiving let your requests be made known to God." We don't have to pretend that we feel OK if we don't. We don't have to lie. God will see through it if we try to fake things anyway. But what we can do is, "let our requests be known to Him". In other words, tell Him all we are sensing. BUT, we need to do this in a certain spirit. We need to do it with an added ingredient. Did you notice what it was? Yes, it is *thankfulness*. Even in the midst of fear we can show gratitude to God. This might look a bit like this:

"Thank you, God, that even though I feel uneasy and frightened right now, you promise that you are with me. Thank you that I don't have to hide that I am feeling troubled, but I can trust that your power is greater. Thank you that even now I can choose to hold on to the truth that you are working this situation out for my good."

Can you see how you are being honest, but with a foundation of thankful faith? There are other spiritual exercises in the following chapter that I hope you will find useful to practice too.

6. Next, we see the result of praying like this. The passage says, "And the peace of God, which surpasses all understanding,

will guard your hearts and your minds in Christ Jesus." God knows that anyone suffering with OCD needs peace. Not just in the heart, but peace in the mind too. An end to the constant worry and fear, and for anxious thoughts to subside and lose their authority. I have written before in my book *In Security* about the kind of peace God gives us. It doesn't just sit over our minds like a blanket. It stands watch at the door of our heads and hearts, waiting for attacks to overcome. God's peace is active and able to break the power of anything we are feeling.

7. Finally, we see the last part of this verse end with the request, "Brothers, whatever is true, whatever is honorable, whatever is just, whatever is pure, whatever is lovely, whatever is commendable, if there is any excellence, if there is anything worthy of praise, think about these things."

This last sentence is very precious to me. When I was made Headgirl of my school many years ago, my Head Teacher asked me to read this passage in the first assembly I led. I can still remember how nervous I was, standing up there in my suit and gown, fumbling my way through these words. But I couldn't think of a better goal for people to think about. Good and godly thoughts make people happy. More than this, they make us better! The Bible says that, *"Pleasant words are like a honeycomb, sweet to the soul and healing to the bones"* Proverbs 16:24 (NET)

In his children's book, *The Twits*, Roald Dahl wrote,

"If a person has ugly thoughts, it begins to show on the face. And when that person has ugly thoughts every day, every week, every year, the face gets uglier and uglier until you can hardly bear to look at it. A person who has good thoughts cannot ever be ugly. You can have a wonky nose and a crooked mouth and a double chin and stick-out teeth, but if you have good thoughts it will shine out of your face like sunbeams and you will always look lovely."

I love that!

If we think about good, excellent and praiseworthy things it will show. Our minds will be healthy, thriving and wonderful places for God's dreams to thrive and flourish. We will be pleasant people to talk to and pray with. We will be joyful, light-hearted and well-intentioned.

Be honest. Is that how you would describe yourself right now?

How are you doing?

If you have a compulsive addiction you may have found that last section very hard to read. You may be thinking that I don't understand what you have gone through, that my words are too simplistic and don't get to the heart of your problems and issues.

I am sorry you feel that way. But I want you to remember something.

God does see exactly what you feel and why. More than this, He understands how you got this way.

Please don't ignore that He might be talking to you now, even through the poverty of my words, and challenging some of your beliefs about yourself.

Write down some of what you are thinking and feeling.

If you are reading this because someone you love is battling OCD, what could you be praying for them as a result of what you have read?

What could you encourage them to do?

How could you stand with them in that?

Remember that because we are both physical *and* spiritual, any addiction we have is going to affect us in all areas of our lives. If you are to begin to understand your own struggles with OCD, you need to take into account both your *brain* and how it is thinking, and your *spirit* and how it is feeling. In any path towards addiction recovery we have to take a holistic approach to getting well.

If your OCD symptoms are really debilitating, you might find it helpful to go and see a GP who may recommend another specialist for you. Your doctor may propose some kind of medication for you. Be aware that some of these may give you side effects, so be careful to discuss these possibilities with your doctor.

You may also be offered some kind of Cognitive Behavior Therapy (CBT). Many people with OCD say this is a most effective way of helping them overcome their problems. CBT can help people to learn a coping technique, which enables them to take their fears less seriously, giving them other options for release.

As with any addiction it won't surprise us to learn that the more we struggle with obsessions and compulsions, the stronger those neural pathways become. The longer we feed and nurture those fears, the more engrained those beliefs will be. But, if we tackle not just the symptoms, but also the triggers and roots of our obsessions, we can change those entrenched patterns of thinking.

Here are some ways you can start to tackle the roots of your issues:

1. Speak to a strong Christian leader or friend about your fears and ask them to pray for you. Galatians 6:2 (NLT) says that we should, *"Share each other's burdens, and in this way obey the law of Christ."* Don't suffer in silence or shame any longer. You don't have to live with your brain warring with you any more. You can be set free! Imagine what that would feel like!

2. Medicate your mind with the word of God. Read through some of the Psalms. Start with Psalm 23 and Psalm 139. Write down each time God shows you His power, His protection and His purposes for you. Re-read those things and repeat them BEFORE worry has a chance to strike. (Then read others Psalms like 46, 62, 91, 104, and 121 in the same way).

3. Tell God how you are feeling. Pray out loud, or in your heart. Jeremiah 33:3 (ESV) tells us, *"Call to me and I will answer you, and will tell you great and hidden things that you have not known."*

4. Meditate on God's love for you. Remind yourself that nothing, not even the worst thing you can possibly imagine, can ever separate you from His love (see Romans 8:28-39). Tell yourself the truth that you are the child of the living God and that His favour rests on you – whether you feel strong or weak (see Galatians 4-4-7; 1 John 3:1).

5. Write down the blessings in your life. Even if they are small, collate them all. Then offer those things to God and remind yourself of all that He has given you. Choose to think about those things more often in your day. Psalm 31:19 (The Message) says, *"What a stack of blessing you have piled up for those who worship you."*

6. Notice when a thought comes into your mind that is contrary to your belief in God. Go to Him with that thought. Ask Him to fill you with trust and confidence in Him instead. Choose to take that thought hostage, as it says in 2 Corinthians 10:5 (NIV):

> *"We demolish arguments and every pretension that sets itself up against the knowledge of God, and we take captive every thought to make it obedient to Christ."*

7. Wait it out. Every time you choose not to act out a compulsive behaviour, you will weaken the obsessive cycle you are in. If you try to wait 20 minutes and distract yourself in another healthy way, your craving will pass. If you keep doing this, you will lessen both the frequency and the power of your obsessive thoughts. They will literally begin to lose their hold on you! I love the verse in Exodus 14:13-14 (NIV) where Moses says to the people,

> *"Do not be afraid. Stand firm and you will see the deliverance the Lord will bring you today. The Egyptians you see today you will never see again. The Lord will fight for you; you need only to be still."*

8. Shorten your rituals. Or change them. Prove to yourself that no harm comes to you when you only wash your hands for 20 seconds rather than a minute. Or do it differently. Try and show yourself that your habits don't need to be fixed or fixated upon. Proverbs 3:5 (NLT) says, *"Trust in the Lord with all your heart; do not depend on your own understanding."*

9. Ask God what good things He has planned for you to do. Try and focus on them instead. Ephesians 2:10 (NIV) tells us that, *"..we are God's handiwork, created in Christ Jesus to do good works, which God prepared in advance for us to do."* Ask God what He has prepared in advance for you to achieve today.

10. Fess up when you mess up! We will have days as addicts where we get taken over. We will realise too late that we have succumbed to compulsive behaviour again. Rather than give up, we need to own up and allow God to forgive us and pour His love out on us again. As Zig Ziglar said, "People often say that motivation doesn't last. Neither does bathing. That's why we recommend it daily." We need to practice living in freedom and cleanliness of heart as an offering each day.

"For we do not have a high priest who is unable to empathize with our weaknesses, but we have one who has been tempted in every way, just as we are—yet he did not sin. Let us then approach God's throne of grace with confidence, so that we may receive mercy and find grace to help us in our time of need." Hebrews 4:15-16 (NIV)

A few final thoughts

I know that overcoming addictive compulsions is a tough road. But I also know that God promises to help us face our fears and doubts and be people who live in full and total freedom. I am praying for you now that God will help you break out of your addictive patterns of thinking and acting and that He gives you a renewed mind today. Remember this truth:

"Though no one can go back and make a brand new start, anyone can start from now and make a brand new ending." (Carl Bard)

I am so happy you chose to read this book and dwell on these truths. I pray that they impact you for the rest of your days and help you live the life you were made for.

Focus On Your Recovery
You may like to meditate on these wonderful promises of restoration that God gives us.

God says he will restore...

1. Our peace and security. *"I will heal my people and will let them enjoy abundant peace and security."* (Jeremiah 33:6 NIV)

2. Our joy and willingness to change. *"Restore to me the joy of your salvation and grant me a willing spirit, to sustain me."* (Psalm 52:12 NIV)

3. Our health. *"'But I will restore you to health and heal your wounds,' declares the Lord."* (Jeremiah 30:17 NIV)

4. Our wasted years. *"I will repay you for the years the locusts have eaten."* (Joel 2:25 NIV)

5. Our plenty. *"You will have plenty to eat and be satisfied and praise the name of the Lord your God, who has dealt wondrously with you."* (Joel 2: 26 NIV)

6. Our wisdom. *"The law of the Lord is perfect, refreshing the soul. The statutes of the Lord are trustworthy, making wise the simple."* (Psalm 19:7 NIV)

7. Our hope. *"There is surely a future hope for you, and your hope will not be cut off."* (Proverbs 23:18 NIV)

8. Rest for the soul. *"Take my yoke upon you and learn from me, for I am gentle and humble in heart, and you will find rest for your souls."* (Matthew 11:29 NIV)

9. Our lives. *"He will renew your life and sustain you in your old age."* (Ruth 4:15 NIV)

10. Our energy. *"But those who hope in the Lord will renew their strength. They will soar on wings like eagles; they will run and not grow weary, they will walk and not be faint."* (Isaiah 40:31 ESV)

- Which of these promises are you most in need of today?
- What could you ask of the Lord today regarding your restoration?

Lastly, you might want to pray this prayer with me:

"Lord Jesus, thank you for journeying with us in our weaknesses. Thank you for being our constant companion and guide. Thank you that your love for us is not dependent on us giving up what we depend on. We pray for one another in our failures and imperfections, that we would never agree to live lives of restriction or isolation.

Help us be real with You, ourselves and others and show our true selves to trusted friends.

Help us walk away from lies that bind us, chains that hold us back and fears that twist who we really are.

May we turn our search for pleasure into a greater search for You.

Help us not to look for permanent joy in anything temporary.

Thank you for those two words you spoke to Your friends: *"Follow me."* Help us do that more and more. Amen."

Please do get in touch with me if you would like to share your experiences of getting free from addiction. The next chapter gives you some short spiritual exercises to help you start or continue on your recovery journey.

So much love, always,

Ems x

Chapter 9
Exercises and Thoughts for Habit Breaking

Excercise 1
"I need you Jesus" – for those at crisis point

Take some time to sit still and try to relax. Try and breathe deeply, but naturally.
Open your hands.
Say out loud:
"Jesus, I need You. I know you are here. Please come and show me yourself."
Now sit and wait a while.
You might want to say that phrase again.
"Jesus, I need You. I know you are here. Please come and show me yourself."

Then, when you are ready, say,
"Jesus, I am physically weak,
please strengthen me.
I am mentally exhausted,
please help me think clearly.
I am at my lowest,
please lift my head.
I feel as though I have failed.
Please forgive me.

Now wait for the Lord to offer you what He wants to give you. When you are ready, say,

"Jesus please exchange my heaviness and despair for your lightness and hope."

Hold your open hands out and up to Jesus and feel the weight of your emotions being lifted.

"Thank you, Jesus, that you have shown me that I can be free."

Repeat this phrase, gently until you feel you can truly mean it.

"Thank you, Jesus, that you have shown me that I can be free."

Now, say this next phrase.

"Jesus, Thank you that you give me all I need for a life of freedom."

Say this phrase again, slowly and deliberately until you feel you are saying it with genuine faith.

Now wait.

Wait for Him to remind you of His unconditional love for you. Wait for Him to comfort you with His reassurance.

Jesus says to you these amazing words from Matthew 11:28-29 (AMP). Read them out loud:

"Come to Me, all you who labour and are heavy-laden and overburdened, and I will cause you to rest. I will ease and relieve and refresh your souls."

Say that phrase again. Which parts most soothe you today?

"Come to Me, all you who labour and are heavy-laden and overburdened, and I will cause you to rest. I will ease and relieve and refresh your souls."

Now read the next verse.

"Take My yoke upon you and learn of Me, for I am gentle (meek) and humble (lowly) in heart, and you will find rest relief and ease (and refreshment and recreation and blessed quiet) for your souls."

Speak out a prayer of gratefulness to Jesus that He understands how you feel in this moment.

Ask Jesus what He wants you to do as a result of your prayer today.

Exercise 2
Lectio Divina
(a way of reading Scripture for healing and growth)

Read through the following text very slowly. Psalm 139:7-11 (TLB):

"I can never be lost to your Spirit! I can never get away from my God! If I go up to heaven, you are there; if I go down to the place of the dead, you are there. If I ride the morning winds to the farthest oceans, even there your hand will guide me, your strength will support me. If I try to hide in the darkness, the night becomes light around me."

• When you are struck by a word or a phrase, stop.
• Stay with the words that moved you, maybe repeating them slowly, allowing them to sink into your heart. Only move on when you are ready to.
• Try to have an inner stillness so that you can perceive the gentle action of God.
• What is one word or phrase the Holy Spirit is impressing

on you? Meditate on that.
- Read the passage again. What do you feel? What specific situation in your life does this relate to today?
- Read the passage again.
- What is God's personal invitation for you from the Scripture? You can write down what God may be saying to you or say a prayer of thanks. Or simply rest quietly in God.

Examples of other texts you might use are: Isaiah 43:1-3;Romans 8:14-17, 28-39; 2 Timothy 1:6-10

Exercise 3
Read the following passage, attributed to Mother Teresa

LIFE IS...
Life is an opportunity, benefit from it.
Life is beauty, admire it.
Life is a dream, realise it.
Life is a challenge, meet it.
Life is a duty, complete it.
Life is a game, play it.
Life is a promise, fulfill it.
Life is sorrow, overcome it.
Life is a song, sing it.
Life is a struggle, accept it.
Life is a tragedy, confront it.
Life is an adventure, dare it.
Life is luck, make it.
Life is too precious, do not destroy it.
Life is life, fight for it.

- How do these words make you feel?

- What do you notice about the words that resonates with your life at the moment?
- How could you connect with God about that?
- Is there someone you need to talk to about something missing from your life?
- Is there something you would like to pray or write down as a result of what you are feeling?

Exercise 4
**This is an exercise about letting go of negative voices.
Read the following poem that I wrote about my past.**

My Failure
I asked her not to come with me, but she took no notice.
Begging her to remain behind, I tried to shut the door.
But she tagged along beside me, breathlessly reminding me
of the shameful, cloying secrets that I wore like a wet, black vest.
Cold, shaky and faint of heart, I weakly pushed her to one side,
But she bounced back into the road,
Desperate and more brazen than before.
Yapping at my heels like an angry, hungry wolf, she followed hard.
So I set a trap for her.
I dug a hole in the road ahead.
I filled it with love and forgiveness and compassion and softness.
And when we came to it, I ran across it joyfully.
And my steps were lighter and higher than before.
But she – she fell in.
She was disgusted by the sweet smells of truth and freedom.
Suffocated by the lack of tawdry reminders

and the way blame no longer landed so squarely on my heart.
But she could not climb out. She struggled, seeing she was losing me.
Then I deliberately walked a narrower, steeper path where she could not fit beside me.
Love made me walk more steadily.
Beginning to drown out the whining voice of her taunting fears.
With loud victory songs of my own, I moved faster.
And soon, I looked back and she was, simply,
no longer there.

- What can you relate to in this writing?
- How does it make you feel?
- What do you find helpful or inspiring?
- What buttons does this press for you about your own past?
- What could you do as a result?
- Could you write something about the ways in which you have overcome something hard?

Exercise 5

Look at the picture opposite. Who do you most identify with today?

- Why would you say that is?
- Who would you most like to be on this picture?
- Why?
- Who would you least like to be?
- Why?
- When people think about you, where do you think they would place you on this picture?
- If you could draw something else on this picture, what would it be and why?

Exercise 6
Read the following poem by an unknown author

RISK

To laugh is to risk appearing the fool
To weep is to risk appearing sentimental
To reach out to others is to risk involvement
To expose feelings is to risk exposing your true self
To place your ideas, your dreams, before a crowd is to risk their loss
To love is to risk not being loved in return
To live is to risk dying
To hope is to risk despair
To try is to risk failure
But risks must be taken,
Because the greatest hazard in life is to do nothing.
The person who risks nothing,
Does nothing, has nothing, and is nothing.
They may avoid suffering and sorrow,
But they cannot learn, feel, change, grow, love, live.
Chained by their attitudes, they are a slave,
They forfeited their freedom.
Only the person who risks can be free.

- What do you agree with from this piece of writing?
- What rings true for your life right now?
- How do you feel about taking risks?
- What risks do you think God might be asking you to take this week?
- What are you going to do about them?
- Write a prayer and a "to do" list to help you focus you thoughts.

Exercise 7
For those struggling with OCD

Begin to recognise a thought that is making you feel unpeaceful, anxious or worried.

Name it out loud.

Tell God how you are feeling about this matter. For example:

"Lord, I feel anxious because I haven't checked the door. I am not sure if it is definitely locked or not."

Consider: Just because I am having these thoughts does not mean that I am not safe. Just because I am thinking these things does not mean this is a reliable indication that I am in danger. Even though I want to check the door (or whatever habit you find yourself repeating obsessively) to decrease my anxiety, does not mean I need to. I will choose instead to speak out my trust in God.

"Lord, thank you that you promise in your word to keep me safe. Thank you that you tell me that nothing can separate me from your love in Christ Jesus. I know that I find true safety and security in you alone. I trust you now."

Decide now to refuse to give in to the temptation to check the lock (or the other repeated behaviour.) If you wait long enough, the anxiety you feel should diminish.

Reward yourself in some way for not giving in to your fears! Well done.

Exercise 8
Read the following paragraph by Marianne Williamson

Our Deepest Fear

Our deepest fear is not that we are inadequate. Our deepest

fear is that we are powerful beyond measure. It is our light, not our darkness, that most frightens us.

We ask ourselves, who am I to be brilliant, gorgeous, talented, fabulous? Actually, who are you not to be?

You are a child of God. Your playing small does not serve the world.

There is nothing enlightened about shrinking so that other people won't feel insecure around you.

We are all meant to shine, as children do. We were born to make manifest the glory of God that is within us. It's not just in some of us; it is in everyone.

And as we let our own light shine, we unconsciously give other people permission to do the same. As we are liberated from our own fear, our presence automatically liberates others."

- Why do you think she says that light is frightening?
- Would you agree with that?
- Is that true for you?
- What would your healing allow for others around you and why?

Exercise 9

The Road Not Taken
Two roads diverged in a yellow wood,
And sorry I could not travel both
And be one traveler, long I stood
And looked down one as far as I could
To where it bent in the undergrowth;
Then took the other, as just as fair,
And having perhaps the better claim,
Because it was grassy and wanted wear;

Though as for that the passing there
Had worn them really about the same,
And both that morning equally lay
In leaves no step had trodden black.
Oh, I kept the first for another day!
Yet knowing how way leads on to way,
I doubted if I should ever come back.
I shall be telling this with a sigh
Somewhere ages and ages hence:
Two roads diverged in a wood, and I-
I took the one less traveled by,
And that has made all the difference.
–Robert Frost

- What kind of road do you feel you are on at the moment?
- Is it one that is a blessing to you, or is it destructive in some way?
- What do you think you need to do to get onto another kind of path?
- What would you leave behind?
- How would that make you feel?

Exercise 10
Try the beautiful body exercise on Lily-Jo's website
www.thelilyjoproject.com/body-beautiful

Exercise 11
This is a relaxation exercise based on Psalm 150:6

"Let everything that has breath praise the Lord."
Sit comfortably with your back as straight as it can be.
- Take a couple of deep breaths just to relax
- Just observe the breath

179

- Observe anything else you are feeling
- Give those sensations, worries or anxieties to God.
- Repeat the verse, *"Let everything that has breath praise the Lord"* a number of times.
- Concentrate on your breathing again. Sense your shoulders relaxing
  - It is normal for your mind to wander away from the simplicity of your breath at times
- Finish your exercise with a short prayer

Exercise 12

This is a simple scriptural declaration I have written, based on Psalm 91. I recommend reading this out loud for at least a week – each morning or each evening.

Lord, your word says that if I dwell in your shelter I will find rest in your shadow. Help me to remind myself that you are my refuge and my fortress, my God, in whom I trust. You have promised that you will save me from anything that ensnares me and from things that are deadly to my mind or my body.

I know that you will cover me with your feathers, and that I will find refuge under your wings. Your faithfulness is my shield. I will not fear the terrors of the night, nor the arrows that fly at me by day. I will not be afraid of the poisons that stalk my mind in the early hours, nor plague me at lunchtime. Others may not make it, but I will! I might see others not overcoming. But I will. I will say, "The Lord is my refuge" and I will make the Most High my dwelling,

No harm will overtake me,
no disaster will come near my home.
For He will command his angels concerning me
to guard me in all my ways;

they will lift me up in their hands,
so that I will not strike my foot against a stone.
I will tread on the dangers of the lion and the cobra;
I will trample the things that have beaten me before – the
great lion and the serpent – and I will beat them.

"Because you love me," says the Lord, "I will rescue you;
I will protect you, for you acknowledge me.
You will call on me, and I will answer you;
I will be with you in trouble,
I will deliver you and honour you.
With long life I will satisfy you
and show you my salvation."

APPENDIX A
The 12 Steps (see Chapter 2)

1. We admitted we were powerless over alcohol – that our lives had become unmanageable.
2. Came to believe that a Power greater than ourselves could restore us to sanity.
3. Made a decision to turn our will and our lives over to the care of God as we understood Him.
4. Made a searching and fearless moral inventory of ourselves.
5. Admitted to God, to ourselves, and to another human being the exact nature of our wrongs.
6. Were entirely ready to have God remove all these defects of character.
7. Humbly asked Him to remove our shortcomings.
8. Made a list of all persons we had harmed, and became willing to make amends to them all.
9. Made direct amends to such people wherever possible, except when to do so would injure them or others.
10. Continued to take personal inventory and when we were wrong promptly admitted it.
11. Sought through prayer and meditation to improve our conscious contact with God as we understood Him, praying only for knowledge of His will for us and the power to carry that out.
12. Having had a spiritual awakening as the result of these steps, we tried to carry this message to alcoholics and to practice these principles in all our affairs.

APPENDIX B
Questions to help you assess yourself
(see Chapter 2)

- What things do you turn to for relief that are healthy?
- How could you build on those things?
- What do you recognise as being a trigger for your cravings?
- Why do you think this is? Where might this stem from?
- What brings you comfort in the midst of despair?
- How could you find that comfort outside of unhealthy addictive patterns?
- What behaviours do you like in yourself?
- Which ones would you dread someone else finding out about?
- How many "if only's" have you used in your thinking today?
- What could you say instead?
- How honest are you being with yourself today?
- Have you made comments today like, "Nothing goes right for me, I always fail"?
- How many times today have you replayed a conversation or situation that has pained you? Why have you done that?
- What could you do instead?
- Are you saying one thing to yourself but not really doing it?
- Have you confessed how you are feeling and what you are doing to anyone you trust?
- Are you being supported and helped as you try to change?
- What could you do to help yourself further?
- Are there resources online, or written books or talks you could use to help you?
- Have you seen a health professional about your problems recently (within the last 6 months)? If so, have you done what they recommended?
- Have you told God the extent of your issues?

APPENDIX C
Bible Promises for Recovery
(see Chapter 2)

"Now the Lord is the Spirit, and where the Spirit of the Lord is, there is freedom." (2 Corinthians 3:17)

"Our freedom that we have in Christ Jesus…" (Galatians 2:4)

"So if the Son sets you free, you will be free indeed." (John 8:36)

"For the law of the Spirit of life has set you free in Christ Jesus from the law of sin and death." (Romans 8:2)

"For you were called to freedom, brothers. Only do not use your freedom as an opportunity for the flesh, but through love serve one another." (Galatians 5:13)

"To Him all the prophets bear witness that everyone who believes in Him receives forgiveness of sins through His name." (Acts 10:43)

"We know that our old self was crucified with Him in order that the body of sin might be brought to nothing, so that we would no longer be enslaved to sin. For one who has died has been set free from sin." (Romans 6:6-7)

"God is faithful, and He will not let you be tempted beyond your ability, but with the temptation He will also provide a way of escape, that you may be able to endure it." (1 Corinthians 10:13b)

"But whoever listens to me will dwell secure and will be at ease, without dread of disaster." (Proverbs 1:33)

"For you did not receive the spirit of slavery to fall back into fear, but you have received the Spirit of adoption as sons, by whom we cry, 'Abba! Father!'" (Romans 8:15)

"For God gave us a spirit not of fear but of power and love and self-control." (2 Timothy 1:7)

"In God, whose word I praise, in God I trust; I shall not be afraid. What can flesh do to me?" (Psalm 56:4)

APPENDIX D
Resources for Further Help

Please find some recommended reading and resources below. NB: not all of these are specifically Christian. Please use your discernment when reading.

Resources for addiction in general:
- *Addiction & Grace*, Gerald G. May (Harper Collins, 2007)
- *Addiction & Virtue*, Kent Dunnington (IVP Academic, 2011)
- *Oh Brave New Church*, Mark Stibbe (Longman & Todd, 1995.)
- https://www.addictionhelper.com

Resources for food addictions:
- *Eat and Stay Thin: simple, spiritual, satisfying weight control*, Joyce Meyer (Warner Books, 1999)
- *Weight Loss for Christians – extraordinarily simple ways to conquer cravings*, Sherry Elaine Evans (Gospel Life 2012)
- *Healthy by Design – weight loss God's way*, Cathy Morenzie (CreateSpace Independent Publishing Platform 2008)
- http://www.danielplan.com (A holistic Bible, fitness and diet guide)
- http://www.oagb.org.uk (Over-eaters Anonymous)

Resources for gambling addictions:
- http://christians-in-recovery.org/Issues_Addiction_Gambling
- *Gambling Addiction: The problem, the pain, and the path to recovery*, John M. Eades (Vine Books 2003)
- *Gambling Facts and Fictions: The anti-gambling handbook to get yourself to stop gambling, quit gambling or never start gambling*, Stephen Katz (Authorhouse 2004)
- *Letting God – revised edition: Christian meditations for recovery,*

A. Philip Parham (HarperOne; Revised ed. Edition 2000)
• *A Hunger for Healing: The twelve steps as a classic model for Christian spiritual growth*, J. Keith Miller (Harper Collins 2011)

Resources for sexual addictions:
• *A Couples Guide to Sexual Addiction*, Paldrom Collins and George Collins (Adams Media, 2011)
• *Erotic Intelligence*, Alexandra Katehakis (HCI, 2010)
• *Hope After Betrayal – Healing when sexual addiction invades your marriage*, Meg Wilson (Kregel Publications, 2007)
• *Out of the Shadows – Understanding sexual addiction*, Patrick Carnes (Hazelden Publishing, 2001)
• *Sex Addiction – The partner's perspective*, by Paula Hall (Routledge, 2015)
• *Understanding and Treating Sex Addiction* by Paula Hall (Routledge, 2012)
• *Your Brain on Porn - Internet pornography and the emerging science of addiction*, Gary Wilson (Commonwealth Publishing, 2015)
• *Your Sexually Addicted Spouse – How partners can cope and heal*, Barbara Steffens and Marsha Means (New Horizon Press Publishers Inc, 2009)
• *Wired for Intimacy – How pornography hijacks the male brain*, William Struthers (IVP Books, 2009)

www.click2kick.com
These are online recovery groups for people who want to stop using porn. They are facilitated by trained mentors in the field. The groups are provided online and consist of 8 x 1 hour sessions. There is no fixed fee but a donation to *The Naked Truth Project* is requested.

www.paulahall.co.uk
Information and video resources explaining sex and porn

addiction and information on our individual, partner and couple services that can be provided via video conferencing. At *www. paulahall.co.uk/form* you'll find our free advice message boards which are run by people in recovery as well as our therapists.

www.sexaddictionhelp.co.uk
A free online self-help tool for sex and porn addiction, created by Paula Hall

www.thenakedtruthproject.com
Naked Truth is the flagship initiative of *Visible* (www. visibleministries.com) and seeks to open eyes and free lives from the damaging impact of pornography through awareness, education and recovery programmes.

Resources for substance addictions
• *The Heart of Addiction: A biblical perspective*, Mark E. Shaw, (Focus Publishing, 2008)
• *Relapse: Biblical prevention strategies*, Mark E. Shaw (Focus Publishing, 2011)
• *Addictions: A banquet in the grave: finding hope in the power of the gospel (resources for changing lives)*, Edward T. Welch, (P & R Publishing, 2001)
• *Chasing the Dragon*, Jackie Pullinger (Hodder and Stoughton 2006)
• http://www.nhs.uk/livewell/addiction/Pages/addictionhome.aspx

Resources for OCD addiction:
• *Can Christianity Cure Obsessive-Compulsive Disorder? A psychiatrist explores the role of faith in treatment*, Dr Ian Osborn (Brazos Press, 2008)
• *OCD – The Erp Cure: 5 Principles and 5 Steps to Turning Off OCD*, Dr Christian R. Komor, (Createspace 2012)

Resources for confidence and emotional health:
• *In Security – living a confident life*, Ems Hancock (River Publishing & Media Ltd, 2015)
• *Overcoming Sinful Anger: How to master your emotions and bring peace to your life*, Fr. T. Morrow, T.G. Morrow, (Sophia Institute Press 2015)
• *Approval Addiction*, Joyce Meyer (Warner Faith, 2005)
• *Change Your Words, Change Your Life*, Joyce Meyer (Hodder and Stoughton, 2012)
• *Mindset: How you can fulfil your potential*, Carol Dweck (Robinson, 2012)
• *Break Out! 5 keys to go beyond your barriers,* Joel Osteen (FaithWords, 2013)
• http://www.thelilyjoproject.com. A website written by trained counsellor Lily-Jo for those experiencing mental health issues.

Help with financial crisis:
https://capuk.org. *Christians Against Poverty* is passionate about releasing people from a life sentence of debt, poverty and their causes.

Bible:
The Life Recovery Bible – Stephen Arteburn and David Stoop (Tyndale House, 2012)

APPENDIX E
Mentoring Questions for Myself

- Am I using my time wisely?
- Am I taking anything for granted?
- Do I have a healthy perspective on my life?
- Am I grateful to God for all He has given me?
- Am I living true to myself?
- Am I waking up in the morning ready to take on the day?
- Am I thinking negative thoughts before I fall asleep?
- Am I putting enough effort into my relationships?
- Am I taking care of myself physically/mentally and spiritually?
- Am I letting matters that are out of my control stress me out?
- Am I achieving the goals that I've set for myself?
- Who am I really?
- What worries me most about the future?
- If this were the last day of my life, would I want to do what I am about to do today?
- What am I really scared of?
- Am I holding on to something I need to let go of?
- If not now, then when?
- What matters most in my life?
- What am I doing about the things that matter most in my life?
- Have I done anything lately worth remembering?
- What legacy am I leaving in my family/business/endeavours?
- Have I made someone smile today?
- What have I given up on?
- When did I last push the boundaries of my comfort zone?
- What small act of kindness was I once shown that I will never forget?
- What do I need to change about myself?
- How many of my friends would I trust with my life?

- Who has had the greatest impact on my life?
- What do I want most in life?
- What is God calling me to do?
- What's the one thing I'd like others to remember about me at the end of my life?
- Does it really matter what others think about me?
- To what degree have I actually controlled the course my life has taken?
- How do I spend most of my time?
- Is this where I thought I would end up?
- What is my biggest weaknesses?
- What is my biggest strength?
- What am I most proud of?
- How do other people see me?
- Am I happy about my reputation?

Think about the word FORM. Form is an acronym for Family, Occupation, Recreation, and Motivation, and it represents four universal areas we can grow in.

In what area can I grow in most this year? How will I do this?

About the Author

Ems Hancock is a speaker and author based in South Manchester. She is married to Jon who is a TV producer. They have 4 children under 12.

Ems' passion is to see people freed to live the way they were intended to. She spends most of her time bringing up the children, writing, and running a listening service in a local secondary school. She and her husband have recently joined a small team to plant a new church as part of the Ivy network of churches. You can find out more about her at:

www.emshancock.com